# CRIMES AND PUNISHMENT

# VOLUME 17

**THE SYMPHONETTE PRESS**
(A Service of Longines-Wittnauer, Inc.)
Robert G. Bartner          President


**PRODUCTION SUPERVISION**
Stonehouse Press


**PHOEBUS PUBLISHING COMPANY**

| | |
|---|---|
| John Paton | Managing Editor |
| Angus Hall | Editor |
| Robin Willcox | Deputy Editor |
| Don Mason | Production Director |


**EDITORIAL PRESENTATION**
Jackson Morley


**ADVISORY EDITORIAL BOARD**
H. Montgomery Hyde
Colin Wilson
C. H. Rolph
J. H. H. Gaute
Nigel Morland

# CONTENTS

CRIME ABOVE THE CLOUDS ............................... 9
   The Hindenburg ......................................... 16
   The $500,000 Drop .................................... 23

SCARLET WOMEN ........................................ 31
   Operation Madame Kitty ............................ 36
   The War-Time Ripper ............................... 45

THE CRIME BUSTERS—
   Murder Under a Microscope ...................... 53

IMPEACHMENT ........................................... 57
   'High Crimes and Misdemeanours'............... 64
   An Old Colonial Score .............................. 73

THE CRIME BUSTERS—
   Angels From Hell ................................... 79

CANNIBALISM .......................................... 83
   Hunger for Human Flesh ........................... 88
   A Mild-Mannered Monster ........................ 96

THE CRIME BUSTERS—
   A Few Mortal Remains ............................ 105

TERROR BY GASLIGHT .............................. 109
   The Killer With a Thousand Faces ............ 115
   Maddened by Greed .............................. 123

A—Z OF CRIME ....................................... 131
   Theft .................................................. 131
   Third Degree ........................................ 133
   Torquemada ......................................... 135
   Tower of London .................................... 137
   Tranby Croft ......................................... 139

Suddenly, in the 1970s, impeachment is very much in the news. It is fitting, therefore, that it is the subject of one of the major themes in Volume 17 of CRIMES AND PUNISHMENT.

It was in March 1868 that Andrew Johnson became the first President of the United States to be impeached for "high crimes and misdemeanours in office", and then tried before a 54-man jury of the Senate.

Johnson was appointed the United States' 17th President after the assassination of Abraham Lincoln. The indictment, which followed three years later, shocked Johnson's Democratic followers, who admired him for several reasons—including the fact that he was not only self-made but self-educated. And it was partly these attributes that led to his being attacked as a "corrupt trickster".

Staying in the nineteenth century, we turn to the subject of Crimes by Gaslight, the era when much of Britain was lit by the mysterious, flickering light of gas. And when such criminals as the master burgler Charles Peace (a capable violin player and an expert at disguising himself) was able to steal — and kill — under cover of darkness.

Coming right up to date—in subject at least—we take a cool, dispassionate look at the subject of Cannibalism . . . one of society's most repulsive acts. In certain cases, however—such as the plane crash in the Andes in 1973, when the survivors had to eat the flesh of their dead friends and comrades in order to stay alive—it has been a necessary factor of survival.

This was not quite the case, however, in the Sierra Nevada in the winter of 1846, when a group of pioneer Americans found themselves trapped by the snow. The so-called Donner Party (led by a former Illinois farmer, George Donner) claimed to have been reduced to cannibalism to save themselves from starvation, but a resulting investigation revealed more sinister circumstances.

There was some public sympathy for Donner and his companions, but none at all for the monstrous American grandfather, Albert Fish, who ate flesh for the perverted thrill it gave him. His trial and bizarre execution—that of a "cannibal extraordinary"—was the talk of America in 1934.

Air Crimes—from the sabotage of the German dirigible *Hindenburg* to a dramatic case of hijacking—and Scarlet Women—prostitutes who were killed or became involved in other serious crimes — make up the other dominant themes in this volume.

The balance is completed by the Crime Busters—featuring such social phenomena as the Hell's Angels gangs. And the A—Z of Crime looks at the birth and practice of that dubious method of police interrogation, the Third Degree.

THE EDITOR

# CRIME ABOVE THE CLOUDS

Men and women like Amy Johnson (above) have gone down in history for their record-breaking feats in aeroplanes. But so have air criminals like Donald Hume (left), Raymond Anthony (in glasses) and Japanese suicide pilots.

TWENTY-FIVE-MILE-AN-HOUR winds lashed across the beach at Kitty Hawk on the morning of December 17, 1903, when Orville Wright clambered between the two wings of his clumsy, kite-like monstrosity and lay flat on his stomach. He slipped the rope that held back the "kite", and the machine surged forward, lurched heavily, then suddenly swooped 10 feet into the air. For the next 10 seconds it wobbled up and down as Orville tried to control the rudder; then the nose pointed down, and it crashed into the sand. Orville jumped off, unhurt. The first motor-driven aeroplane had carried a human being just over 100 yards, and the twentieth century had really arrived.

Even today, when we are thoroughly blasé about monster jets that can carry hundreds of passengers at more than 1000 miles an hour, the story of those early days of flying makes some of the most exciting reading in the world. It had to happen, of course, once man had noticed that a box-kite could sail for long distances through the air, and when Otto invented the internal combustion engine in 1877 it was inevitable that some genius would think of combining the engine with the box kite to make an aeroplane.

**Vast ransoms**

The great pioneer Otto Lilienthal stood on a hilltop in 1891 and leapt into the air, suspended from a kind of kite that made him look like an enormous bat; he planed smoothly down to the bottom of the hill, steering the kite by means of rudders. The two Wright brothers, Orville and Wilbur—who ran a cycle business in Dayton, Ohio—read about Lilienthal's gliding feats in 1896 and were feverishly excited. Lilienthal broke his neck in his "glider"; so did the great English pioneer, Percy S. Pilcher. Undeterred, the Wright brothers worked on the problem of how to combine a glider and an engine, and they solved it that morning of December 17, 1903—surely one of the great days in human history.

Every major technical advance has brought its own kind of crime. The horse was first used by Mongol hordes to prey on peaceful rural communities; sea-faring brought sea raiders like the Vikings and the pirates of the Mediterranean; and the railways inspired Jesse James to invent train robbery. The aeroplane, in its turn, has led to the development of a wide and peculiar variety of crimes, from international air-smuggling to the form of air piracy known as sky-jacking. Bank robbers have escaped in aeroplanes, murderers have thrown bodies from aeroplanes,

**EPOCH MAKERS . . . The Wright brothers were first in the air. Right and centre left: Two versions of their biplane. Above and far right: Pioneer Amy Johnson.**

Keystone

Keystone

Science Museum

and sky-jackers have parachuted from aeroplanes, carrying vast ransoms for the lives of the passengers. It is becoming increasingly clear that, if air crime is not to become one of the most serious problems of the future, there will have to be firm and concerted action by every civilized country in the world.

Yet even half a century ago such a thought would have been inconceivable. Five years after the Wright brothers made their first flight, the prophet of science, H. G. Wells, wrote a novel called *The War in the Air* in which he described aerial "dog fights", and bombing from an aeroplane. But no one took this seriously; it was just another example of Wells's grotesque imagination. Even well-informed people believed that the aeroplane would never be anything more than a scientific toy, like Edison's phonograph. Even Blériot's cross-Channel flight in 1909 did little to change that view. It was the dirigible balloon that was regarded as the great aerial hope of the future, at least until the First World War. Then it was the aeroplanes that did the real damage and helped to change the course of the war.

**Futility**

The war ended; the jazz age came and went, and it seemed that the underworld had overlooked the aeroplane as a potential instrument of crime. But one imaginative young American, Harry Crosby, saw it as a spectacular means of suicide. Rich, good-looking and cultured, Crosby had no reason to want to die. But he had seen many of his friends die in the war, and he had more money than was good for him. Living in Paris during that period of futility and boredom described by Hemingway in *The Sun Also Rises*, Harry and his beautiful wife Caresse decided that they would commit suicide by aeroplane on a predetermined date, October 31, 1942.

They would do this by taking the aircraft up over the jungles of Brazil and flying it straight into the sun until they ran out of fuel. Crosby was obsessed by the sun. But when he actually committed suicide, on December 10, 1929, it was in a less original manner. He and his mistress —a society woman, Mrs. Josephine Bigelow—went to a studio in the Hotel des Artistes in New York, and there both died by shooting themselves through the head. So Crosby lost the chance of becoming the world's first air suicide.

That distinction probably goes to the first Japanese "kamikaze" pilot, Admiral Masubumi Arima, who, on October 15, 1944, crashed his Zero fighter into the U.S.S. *Franklin* off the Philippine island of Luzon. Arima's action started a virtual epidemic of suicide by kamikaze pilots, whose reckless bravery came close to turning the war in the Pacific in favour of Japan.

But for a time there was another possible candidate for the doubtful honour of being the world's first aerial suicide. This was the ex-R.A.F. officer Bill Lancaster, whose strange disappearance was preceded by his trial on a charge of murder. Bill Lancaster, born in 1898 near Birmingham, England, entered the R.A.F. towards the end of the 1918 war, and left the service in 1926. He decided to try for a long-distance flying record to Australia in a new light plane, the Avro Avian.

**In love**

Three weeks before the flight he met a pretty Australian journalist, Mrs. "Chubbie" Miller, who begged him to allow her to go with him. They set out in October 1927. Bad weather forced a crash landing in Sumatra, and they arrived in Port Darwin in March 1928. Another pilot, Bert Hinkler, had passed them in another Avro Avian, so the Lancaster-Miller team failed to gain their record for the longest flight in a light plane. But they had one consolation: they were in love.

Their affair continued for the next four years, during which time Lancaster worked in America as a free-lance flier. And although he remained in love with Chubbie, she had ceased to love him. In March 1932 Bill and Chubbie were living together in Miami, Florida, and Lancaster went away on a flying trip, leaving Chubbie together with a young airman-journalist named Haden Clarke, who was collaborating with her on her autobiography. Clarke was a weakling and a neurotic, and—like Lancaster—he aroused protective feelings in Chubbie. Soon they were having a love affair. She wrote to Lancaster to tell him that she had decided to marry Clarke.

**Whitest man**

Lancaster was shattered, although he did his best to behave like a gentleman. He telegraphed them, asking them to delay the wedding "until he could come and be best man", and got home as soon as he could. It was April 13, 1932. The three had not been together long when Lancaster told Haden Clarke that he had betrayed his trust. Clarke blustered furiously. Finally, Chubbie and Clarke agreed to postpone their marriage for a month, to give them time to think it over.

Lancaster and Clarke slept in camp beds on the verandah, and by the time they fell asleep they had made up the quarrel. Clarke's last words were: "You're the whitest man I know." In the middle of the night there was the sound of a shot, and Lancaster banged on Chubbie's door. Clarke, he said, had shot himself—and, worse still, had used a gun that he, Lancaster, had bought in St.

Louis just before flying back to Miami.

There were two suicide notes, both typewritten, but signed by Clarke, and a suicide verdict was returned at the inquest. But a week later a handwriting expert declared that the signatures on the suicide notes were forged. Bill Lancaster and Mrs. Miller were arrested, but she was released almost immediately. Lancaster admitted forging the suicide notes, but he insisted that Clarke's death had been suicide, all the same.

## Bigamous wife

The case against Lancaster looked black. His story was that he had wakened up and found Clarke dying from the gunshot wound in his head. Realizing he might be accused of murder, he had rushed out, typed the suicide notes, and tried to get the dying Clarke to sign them. Clarke was too weak, and Lancaster had done it.

When the defence counsel began to investigate Haden Clarke's background, however, they unearthed evidence that made the suicide seem altogether more likely. Clarke was not only married already, but had also a second—bigamous—wife. He was something of a confidence man, and was a drug addict. The dead man's skull was produced in court, and powder burns were pointed out near the wound. This suggested that the shot *was* self-inflicted; a would-be killer would not risk waking his victim by pressing the gun against his head. Finally, Lancaster was found not guilty.

But he was fully aware that his career was probably ruined; many people thought him guilty. His relationship with Chubbie had not apparently survived the trial; he decided that there was only one way to get back into flying: to break a world record. This time he decided to try to break the speed record from England to the Cape; it had formerly been held by Jim Mollison, but had been broken by Amy Johnson, who was now a universal heroine. If he could break *her* record it would mean certain fame...

## Mummified body

The flight was financed by his father. When he set out on April 11, 1933, he also had the comfort of knowing that Chubbie was prepared to make another effort to live with him when he returned. His task was to try to fly the 6500 miles in less than four days and seven hours. Nearly 36 hours later he took off from Gao in Africa. Then he vanished.

A wide search was mounted. Many people were of the opinion that this was suicide. He was hours behind Amy Johnson, and there was no chance of beating her record. He had been heard to say that, if he failed, he had nothing to live for. If he *was* guilty of Clarke's murder, this

was an additional reason for ending it all in a final crash-dive.

It was nearly 30 years later that the truth finally became known. The French had established an atomic station at Reggan, in the Sahara desert, and in February 1962 a motorized patrol 170 miles south of Reggan found the wrecked aeroplane, and a man's mummified body inside it. Lancaster's diary told the story of engine failure nearly two hours after leaving Reggan. The plane crashed, but he survived for eight days. At one point he saw the flare of a searching aeroplane and fired off one of his own flares. But although he spent the night in a state of euphoric hope, no rescue came. Finally, Bill Lancaster died of thirst.

## Newspaper confession

It was the Second World War that brought the age of air crime altogether closer, and in 1949 Brian Donald Hume, a petty crook who specialized in selling stolen cars, and who had learned to fly in the R.A.F., murdered Stanley Setty, the dealer who supplied them, and hacked his body in several pieces. On October 5, 1949, Hume hired an Auster aeroplane at

Elstree and scattered parts of the body over the English Channel.

The next day he threw the torso out of an aeroplane, but it was washed ashore. Hume was traced through one of the five-pound notes used in Setty's last business transaction, but Hume insisted that he had disposed of the body at the insistence of three gangsters. He was found not guilty of murder, but guilty of being an accessory, and sentenced to 12 years in prison. When he came out in 1958 he wrote a confession of the murder for a Sunday newspaper.

But the priority in aerial murder undoubtedly goes to the French-Canadian Joseph Guay, who, on September 9, 1949, waved goodbye to his wife Rita as she boarded a Dakota of Canadian Pacific Airlines at Quebec. By the time the plane took off, Guay was sweating heavily. He had reason to. Five minutes later, the Dakota exploded in mid-air, killing everyone on board. Guay was one of many

**WAITING FOR DEATH . . . Six pilots are photographed before being sent to die for their country. Below: Two attacks. A direct hit would cause severe damage.**

UPI, Keystone/Quartet

relatives of passengers who streamed to the airport two hours later. He was apparently shattered by the news of the explosion, and broke down so convincingly that kindly onlookers drove him to a hotel. His five-year-old daughter was with him.

**Seared metal**

The plane had exploded over a dense forest near Sault-au-Cochon. Witnesses on the ground had noted that the plane's engines continued running after the explosion; this proved that the engines were not at fault. Twenty-three bodies were recovered from the wreckage. In the luggage compartment the searchers discovered seared metal that indicated that this was where the explosion had taken place, and chemical analysis revealed it was due to dynamite.

The police carefully checked the passenger list, and the list of baggage. One item intrigued them: a crate containing "religious statuary", weighing 26 lbs. No statue had been found in the wreckage. An appeal by the police brought forward a taxi driver who had picked up a woman with a wooden crate on the day of the disaster and driven her to the airport. He was able to give her address.

When the police checked there, they discovered that Marie Petri was in hospital, recovering from an overdose of sleeping tablets. When they called to see her, almost her first words were: "He made me do it." "He" was the jeweller Albert Guay, who had also been her lover — before he discovered a younger and prettier mistress, Marie-Ange Robitaille. She admitted that Guay had asked her to buy dynamite for him, and that her brother, a legless cripple named Generaux, had made a timing mechanism to detonate it.

### Wildly infatuated

Slowly, the incredible story became clear. Guay was a man who could never be contented with one woman. For years, Marie Petri — who worked as a waitress — had been his mistress, and he supported her in a flat. Then, three years earlier, he had met the beautiful 16-year-old Marie-Ange — who preferred to be called Angel Mary — in a nightclub, where she worked as a cigarette girl. He became wildly infatuated with her, and she became his mistress.

When Guay's wife found out, she went to see Marie-Ange's father. As a consequence, Marie-Ange moved out, and Guay installed her in his other mistress's flat. After a few months of torment, the bitterly jealous Marie Petri moved out. Guay now became moody and savage, and Marie-Ange tried to leave him. He caught her on the train and dragged her back to the flat.

### Impossible task

It was probably then that he began to brood on how he might gain a legal hold over her by marrying her. A friend of Guay's, named Lucien Carreau, told how Guay had once offered him 100 dollars to administer poisoned cherry brandy to Rita Guay. He had refused. After the air crash, Guay had called on him and offered him 500 dollars if he would promise to say nothing about the earlier offer — Guay could afford it; his wife had been insured for $10,000. Now thoroughly afraid, Carreau again refused. Guay, who did not like to be crossed, flew into a wild temper: "He was like an animal" — and stormed out.

Guay's trial opened in March 1950. At first there was a certain amount of public sympathy for Marie Petri, who told how Guay called on her after the explosion, told her she was responsible, and dwelt sadistically on how they would hang her. However, when the crippled Generaux Ruest vanished, and had to be found and kept under police supervision to get him into court, there were many who wondered if the brother and sister were less innocent than they seemed.

As far as Guay was concerned, it was an open and shut case; the defence had an impossible task. They tried to insist that a timing mechanism made from an alarm clock would not work; an explosives expert disproved it by constructing one in court from an old alarm clock and making it blow a fuse in front of the jury. When he added that 10 lbs. of dynamite would be enough to destroy any aeroplane, Guay's last hope vanished. He was found guilty and hanged in January 1951. Eighteen months later, Marie Petri and her brother also went to the gallows — new evidence revealed that they had quite willingly

**ILL-FATED LOVERS Chubbie Miller and Bill Lancaster (left). Below: Self-confessed murderer Donald Hume and the man (right) whom he hacked to pieces . . .**

AP, Keystone

Keystone, UPI, Wide World, AP

participated in the plot to blow up the aeroplane. Guay's gruesome descriptions of hanging, which had frightened Marie Petri into attempting suicide, proved to be true after all.

It is not entirely accurate to say that the age of air crime began with the Guay explosion and Hume's flight over the Channel. Ever since the end of the war international gangs had used aeroplanes for smuggling and other criminal operations. The book *Airline Detective* by ex-detective Donald Fish became a bestseller, and formed the basis of the popular television series *Zero One*; it is a brilliant description of the many forms of crime encountered by an airport security man.

### Iron bar

The world's first sky-jacking took place as early as 1947. On July 16 of that year a Chinaman named Wong Yu, together with three other desperadoes, Chiu Tok, Chiu Choi and Chiu Cheng, tried to take over a Catalina flying boat of Cathay Pacific Airlines, flying from Macao to Hong Kong. The intention was straight air-piracy; the flying boat would be taken to a remote place on the Pearl River, the passengers robbed, and some held for ransom. But from the moment the four men flourished guns and ordered the pilots to change course, things went wrong. The co-pilot, a Scotsman named McDuff, grabbed an iron bar and began swiping at the gunmen. Wong Yu fired and killed the pilot, and the plane went into a dive and plunged into the river. Ironically, the only survivor was Wong Yu. In hospital he confided the story of

**ALCOHOLIC SKY-JACKER Raymond Anthony (left), Albert Guay the Canadian pioneer in sabotage (centre), and (above) suicide pact girl Mrs. Josephine Bigelow.**

the hijack to another patient—who was intensely interested, because he happened to be a police officer. Just two weeks after the world's first sky-jack, Wong Yu signed a confession and was executed.

It was in the late 1960s that sky-jacking suddenly became a real menace to world airline safety. Most of the early cases were of planes bound for Miami, Florida, which were ordered by left-wing hi-jackers to fly to Cuba. One man, Raymond Anthony, a middle-aged alcoholic, forced a plane from Baltimore to land in Cuba by threatening the pilot with a penknife, and by that time non-resistance had become so much a part of the airline pilots' policy that he succeeded. However, Cuba expelled him, and he was arrested and sentenced to 15 years in gaol. American sky-jacking has become less popular only as it has become clear that Castro is intensely embarrassed by it, and would prefer not to give refuge to "political exiles"—who are mostly cranks with a desire to get "away from it all".

Similarly, Arab terrorist sky-jacking has diminished as Middle-Eastern countries have showed the same reluctance to allow refuge to the terrorists. It is impossible to doubt that *this* is the only genuine solution to the problem. And, somehow, it is appropriate that the terrorist menace should be creating some kind of unity between all the governments of our divided world.

15

# THE HINDENBURG

The graceful airship *Hindenburg* was acclaimed as a masterpiece of safety, comfort and efficiency. Unfortunately, it was also a symbol of Nazi so-called "supremacy"—a target for sabotage . . .

ALL the omens were there: whether you preferred the factual or the supernatural warning signs, it all added up to the same thing. The most famous aircraft in the world was in deadly danger.

Marie Lehmann, wife of Ernst Lehmann, Captain of the airship *Hindenburg,* begged him not to go on the next flight. She had visited a gipsy clairvoyant in Vienna, and the woman had seen something terrible in the crystal ball. "Your husband is an airship captain," she had said. "But not for long. Warn him not to ride on the *Hindenburg.* I see it on the other side of the ocean. It is in flames."

More down to earth, SS-Sturmbann-fuhrer Karl Hufschmidt called an emergency meeting at his office in Berlin's Wilhelmstrasse, on that spring day of 1937.

"We have reason to believe," he told the three men in front of him, "that a sabotage attempt is to be made on the airship *Hindenburg,* probably after landing in New York from the transatlantic flight leaving today. I have prepared dossiers on all the passengers. Some are definite security risks. It is your duty to watch the movements of everyone on board the airship and to arrest anyone you suspect of being the saboteur."

The three men shifted uncomfortably.

This was not their normal line of duty at all. Colonel Fritz Erdmann, Major Franz Witt and First-Lieutenant Klaus Hinkelbein were all senior Luftwaffe intelligence officers. They had been specially briefed on low-level reconnaissance work. Disguised as passengers, it was their job to locate military installations, factories and tactical landmarks as the airship sailed slowly over France and Britain.

## Political undesirables

"We have no experience of such work; we aren't policemen," protested Colonel Erdmann. The SS-Sturmbannfuhrer silenced him with a bleak look. "Correct me if I am wrong," he said, "but some time ago didn't the Luftwaffe accept all responsibility for the *Hindenburg's* flights, on the grounds that national prestige was involved? Presumably that includes security."

Without waiting for an answer, SS-Sturmbannfuhrer Hufschmidt opened a thick folder and began listing the 36 passengers who had booked for the four-day flight leaving Germany for New York that evening. The Gestapo had obviously been busy. The dossiers were complete down to the last detail.

"The main suspect, in our opinion," said the SS-Sturmbannfuhrer, "is an

American so-called comedian and acrobat named Joseph Spah. This man has spent many years touring Germany, and our reports indicate that he may be more than a mere entertainer. Although he travels as an American, he was born in Germany. He has been known to mix with political undesirables. This man in particular must be kept under constant surveillance. There are other suspects: an American-Jewish fancy-goods importer named Moritz Feibusch — you can never be too careful about Jews — Karl Clemens, a Berlin photographer with a dubious background, and Edward Douglas, an American advertizing executive who is known to us as a secret agent."

The three Luftwaffe officers still weren't convinced. Acrobats, fancy-goods salesmen and suspected American spies didn't sound like the raw material for a sabotage plot. "But what proof have you got that any conspiracy exists?" asked Colonel Erdmann.

"Our undercover agents in New York are quite specific about a time-bomb," said the SS-Sturmbannfuhrer. "Our

**THE THIRD REICH attached a great deal of importance to this prestige project. Nazi supremacy was not just a philosophy — it had to be shown as true.**

Ambassador in Washington, Dr. Hans Luther, has also been warned of a sabotage attempt. The evidence is too conclusive to ignore. In the circumstances, every precaution should be taken. The *Hindenburg* is the pride of Germany, a symbol of the technological strides the Fatherland has made under Adolf Hitler. There must be no accidents!"

The officers saluted and turned to leave; as they reached the door, the SS-Sturmbannfuhrer looked up and gave a tired smile. "If you doubt the reliability of our sources," he said, "you might like to make a note in your diary. We have also received information about another sabotage attempt. We expect Communist terrorists to leave a time-bomb in the Paris-Marseilles express on Wednesday night."

Doubt still lingered in the minds of the three officers as they followed the other passengers up the gangway into the whale-like body of the *Hindenburg* at 7 p.m. that evening. It seemed incredible. Who on earth would wish to blow up the *Hindenburg*? "If you ask me," said First-Lieutenant Hinkelbein, as the airship prepared to cast off, "the whole thing's a false alarm. The SS have just got the jitters."

Colonel Erdmann was not with the other two. He had been called back to the gangway by telephone. Obeying some strange feminine instinct, his wife had broken away from the crowd for a final, tearful embrace. She was still crying as the *Hindenburg* rose gently above Frankfurt airport and headed towards the Atlantic.

## High Mass

The date was Sunday, May 2, 1937. Three days later, on Wednesday, May 5, a bomb exploded on the Bordeaux-Marseilles express as it was travelling at 60 m.p.h., killing one passenger and injuring 20 others. By then, the *Hindenburg* was only one day from New York . . . and the time-bomb had already been placed.

As huge as an ocean liner and as luxurious as a first-class hotel, the *Hindenburg* was the latest and most magnificent of Germany's record-breaking fleet of airships. In Frankfurt, it filled a hangar 1000 feet long and 20 storeys high.

Its vast bulk, strengthened by a framework containing 10 miles of girders, was lifted from the ground as gently as a child's balloon by seven million cubic feet of hydrogen stored in 16 inflatable gas cells. At 80 m.p.h., its progress was so smooth and steady that on its maiden voyage to New York in 1936 the Reverend Paul Schulte was able to celebrate High Mass in the passenger lounge without spilling a drop of the sacrificial wine.

The 75 passengers slept in 25 staterooms on two decks. There were showerrooms, bars, a lounge, library, reading-room, smoking-room and two 130-ft. observation galleries commanding superb views. In the restaurants, waiters served the finest food and wines, prepared in kitchens stocked with 5500 pounds of fresh meat, 22 pounds of fish, 440 pounds of butter and nearly 1000 eggs.

No existing plane could compete with the *Hindenburg* for long-range reliability. The airship could travel 10,000 miles without refuelling and stay in the air for six days. While other countries had scrubbed the airship as obsolete and pinned their future on planes, the Germans continued to improve on the prototype conceived by Count Ferdinand von Zeppelin at the turn of the century.

In every way, the *Hindenburg* was the summit of their achievements. Britain,

CREATOR of the German airship, Count Graf von Zeppelin (left), head of the Zeppelin corporation in 1937. Dr. Hugo Eckener (centre), and (below) the "old buffoon" Field-Marshal von Hindenburg.

France, Italy and America had all suffered disastrous experiences with airships. The British had given up their experiments in a hurry in 1930, after the much-publicized *R-101* crashed in France, killing the Air Minister.

The Germans, however, had carried nearly a million passengers without a single accident. Rigorous safety precautions had eliminated any risk from static electricity or sparks. On one occasion, an airship had been completely covered in the electrical phenomenon known as "St. Elmo's Fire" without any mishap.

### Propaganda instrument

Not that the designers or the crew took any chances; anything that might cause a spark was banned. There were no buttons on the crewmen's tunics. The men wore rubber-soled shoes, from which even the metal eyelets had been removed. On the *Hindenburg's* first transatlantic trip in 1936 it had sailed through a hurricane without any trouble; one of the passengers had been the actor, Douglas

**VICTIM of sabotage, Captain Lehmann (below) had already been warned by his wife . . . Dr. Hans Luther (right), German Ambassador in Washington, kept silent . . .**

Fairbanks, with his wife, formerly Lady Ashley. Throughout the flight he had worn slippers with the glittering initials "DF" in diamonds.

Even Lt.-Comdr. Scott Peck, an official observer for the United States Navy, had come to the conclusion, "I consider all possibilities of danger in the new Zeppelin eliminated." The *Hindenburg's* 1936 season had been a spectacular success, and all cabins were now fully booked for the 18 flights to New York in 1937.

But behind the scenes the *Hindenburg* was shuddering beneath a series of political storms which threatened its entire future. The head of the Zeppelin Corporation—which manufactured and ran the airship fleet—was Dr. Hugo Eckener. A pacifist by nature, Dr. Eckener was inspired by a belief in the power of the airship to promote international trade and understanding between nations. They were noble sentiments, but they flew right in the face of Germany's new masters, the Nazis. To them, the Zeppelin was a unique propaganda instrument; a great, floating symbol of the supremacy of the Third Reich.

Dr. Eckener had already fallen foul of Germany's Minister of Propaganda, Dr. Josef Goebbels, over a Ministry decision to paint the swastika on the tail-fin of the *Graf Zeppelin,* then the biggest airship in the fleet. Dr. Eckener had protested, but Dr. Goebbels had insisted. The Minister had won, and as a parting shot had warned, "Make sure you display the swastika on the new airship, LZ 129."

The LZ 129 was the code-name for the *Hindenburg,* still undergoing flight tests at Frankfurt. Dr. Goebbels already had ideas for the LZ 129. At an impressive launching ceremony it was to be named "Adolf Hitler".

On March 4, 1936, during the LZ 129's final trial flight over Munich, the Mayor of the city radioed Dr. Eckener to ask, "What is the name of your wonderful new airship?" Impulsively, Dr. Eckener answered "The *Hindenburg*".

### Magnet for agitators

Dr. Goebbels was furious. "How dare you name your airship after that grey-haired buffoon of the old regime, Field-Marshal von Hindenburg?" he stormed. "It is an insult to the Fuhrer! Now the whole world knows the airship by its idiotic new name. There is nothing we can do about it now. But I tell you this. In Germany, your airship will only be referred to by its number, LZ 129. And I have given orders that no newspaper shall

ever mention your name in connection with the Zeppelin fleet in general, and the new airship in particular."

Patiently, Dr. Eckener tried to explain that, outside Germany, the combination of scarlet swastikas on the tail and the name "Adolf Hitler" on the nose would probably offend more people than it impressed. It could also act as a magnet for agitators and anti-Nazi demonstrations. Dr. Eckener's misgivings were to be confirmed only too tragically.

### Armed men

Peevishly, Dr. Goebbels issued an order through the puppet "Reich League of Periodical Publishers" banning any mention of Dr. Eckener's name in both newspapers and magazines. At the same time, the Burgomaster of Berlin was told to change the name of "Eckener Avenue" to "Adolf Hitlerstrasse".

With Dr. Eckener safely brought to heel, the Nazis used the *Graf Zeppelin* and *Hindenburg* as airborne circus marquees in a succession of vulgar publicity stunts. During the Rhineland election, the airships, bristling with loudspeakers, hovered over key cities, urging the townsfolk to vote for Hitler. Thousands of tiny parachutes carried propaganda leaflets which proclaimed, "Thirty-seven parties

destroyed Germany in 15 years. One man, the Fuhrer, built it up again in three."

In August, the airships nosed over the Berlin Olympic Stadium so low that the crews could hear the "Seig Heils!" of the huge audience. More uplift was supplied to the inhabitants of the "disputed areas" of Danzig and the Polish Corridor, where loyal German hearts were gladdened by the sound of military marches and slogans bellowing from the *Hindenburg's* loudspeakers. To complete the blissful scene, the sky suddenly rained thousands of tiny Nazi flags, released by the airship's crew.

The incessant propaganda and ballyhoo had now resulted in the very backlash Dr. Eckener had feared. Somehow, a madman inflamed by anti-Nazi feelings threatened to blow his beloved *Hindenburg* out of the sky. Unless the bomb could be discovered first. The crew were the first to realize something was wrong.

Early on the morning of May 2, the first aircraftsmen to report to the Frankfurt hanger found themselves surrounded by armed SD men. "We have been ordered to search the entire airship," said the officer-in-charge. "It is suspected there is a bomb on board." For three hours the SD men searched the intricate cobweb of struts and rigging inside the

**THE EXPLOSION . . . A photographer was waiting to film the arrival of the passengers after their luxury journey. Instead he caught the ship's destruction.**

*Hindenburg,* but nothing was found.

Then it was the turn of the passengers. At the flight assembly point, the Frankfurter Hof Hotel, ruffled passengers had to submit to an unprecedented security check. There were protests and complaints as guards confiscated matches, cigarette lighters, flashlight batteries— even a child's Mickey Mouse toy that gave off sparks. "All your property will be kept safely in separate bags, marked with your name," they were told. "After the trip, we shall return everything, and you may keep the bags as a souvenir, with the compliments of the airline."

### Sheer drop

Only one man was missing from the check, the chief suspect, Joseph Spah. He arrived at the airfield by car, clutching a box wrapped in brown paper. Officials swooped down on him, but the box contained only a Dresden doll for his daughter. He seemed amazed at the consternation he had caused.

From among the passengers, the three Luftwaffe intelligence officers watched the comic little scene being played out. It could be a ruse to divert suspicion, they thought. The SS-Sturmbannfuhrer had been right. Spah needed watching. But within an hour of take-off, Spah had eluded them.

Spah insisted on feeding his dog, an Alsatian puppy, which was being carried in the freight compartment in the rear of the airship. "I understood it would be okay when I booked," he told Captain Lehmann. The Captain had no reason to doubt his word. "Take Mr. Spah to his dog," he told the Chief Steward, Heinrich Kubis. The compartment was in an area normally out of bounds to passengers, reached by a series of linked gangplanks with a sheer drop below to the linen skin of the airship. Although he was an acrobat, Spah seemed nervous. "What if I fell off and hit the bottom?" he asked. "You'd go right through," said Kubis succinctly.

The three Luftwaffe officers were alarmed when they heard of Spah's jaunt through the airship. "We must not let the man out of our sight!" said Colonel Erdmann, but on the following day Spah gave them the slip again. On the pretext of taking a look at his dog, he broke away from a conducted tour of the airship. The leader, the ship's doctor, was powerless

to stop him. "Go ahead," said Spah, "I'll only be a few ticks, and I'll soon catch you up."

That night, Chief Radio Officer Willy Speck awoke from a terrifying nightmare. He dreamt his little son had been placed on a funeral pyre and he had watched as the boy was burned alive. "It was so real," he mumbled to one of his crew-mates, "so real."

## Cheap clock

Joseph Spah was caught, the next day, wandering alone along the catwalk inside the shell of the airship. A member of the crew took him to Chief Steward Kubis, who demanded an explanation. "I just wanted some exercise," said Spah, "and I found one of the rear doors open." Spah's route had taken him once more to the stern of the airship, past Gas Cell No. IV, its canvas pulsing gently like some huge lung.

"The man's had time to plant a dozen bombs!" exploded Colonel Erdmann when he heard the news. "He's a paying passenger," said Major Witt. "We can't follow him round the ship like a criminal."

In the rear of the *Hindenburg,* sewn into the canvas at the base of Gas Cell No. IV, a home-made bomb awaited the careful touch of its creator to set the

timing device. It had been placed there, not by Joseph Spah, but by one of the men even SS-Sturmbannfuhrer Huf-schmidt had dismissed as "completely beyond suspicion".

At dawn on Thursday, May 6, the *Hindenburg* was 350 miles from Boston and eight hours behind schedule. There was no chance of it landing at the airfield at Lakenhurst, New Jersey, at the advertized time of 6 a.m. To streamline landing arrangements, it had been agreed that any airship missing the morning touch-down would have to wait until 6 p.m. But even this landing-time now seemed doubtful. Heavy winds had slow-ed down the *Hindenburg,* and it wasn't until 4 p.m. that the airship appeared over Lakenhurst — only to run head-on into the path of a storm. To the west was a grey and ugly cliff of cloud, streaked with lightning. The Captain dropped a mes-sage attached to a weight to the ground crew below. "Riding out the storm," it said.

The *Hindenburg* edged gently towards the Jersey coast and away from the

**WITHIN MINUTES the *Hindenburg* was reduced from a gleaming triumph of human technology to a smoking wreck — not un-like other symbols of Nazi ambition . . .**

Wide World/Quartet

approaching storm clouds. At 5.35 p.m. Lakenhurst radio control advised them that weather conditions were not yet suitable for landing. Just before 6 p.m. a pair of hands swiftly cut through the fabric of Gas Cell No. IV and reached for the bomb. Deftly, the hands set the timer to detonate in two hours' time, at 8 p.m. The hands replaced the bomb and arranged the folds at the base of the container to disguise the tear. The bomb was not an explosive but an incendiary device.

When the phosphorus burned away the canvas sufficiently, the hydrogen and the incoming oxygen would ignite. By then, the *Hindenburg* would have landed and the passengers be safely clear of the explosion. The lives of everyone on board the *Hindenburg* were now governed by the cheap clock inside the fabric of Gas Cell No. IV;

At 6.12 p.m. Lakenhurst radioed clearance to land, but it was not until 6.44 that the *Hindenburg* altered course above Forked River towards the airfield.

### Orange flame

On the ground, more than 200 men were deployed for the docking and landing routine. As the *Hindenburg* settled down over the airfield, a line of men spaced out in a rough outline of the airship waited for the landlines to be thrown down and secured. A 75-foot mast built on to a railroad waggon manoeuvred into position. The nose of the airship would be drawn by a steel cable into a homing-cone on top of the mast, like a bull with a ring in its nose. Another railroad waggon waited to winch down the tail of the

**RESCUERS made frantic attempts to help the passengers trapped inside the airship. There were some miraculous escapes — but the saboteur was killed.**

airship. The time was 7.15 p.m.

Four minutes later, the *Hindenburg* had been nursed to a dead stop 200 feet above the ground and directly above the homing-cone. At 7.21 the landing lines spun out like streamers and spiralled to the ground. The hands that had set the timing-device began to sweat. The *Hindenburg* was well behind time. Even if nothing went wrong, there were only 39 minutes to go.

Everything happened at once. In the stern of the airship, Gas Cell No. IV gave a gasp as if hit in the stomach. A wavering orange flame lit up the inside of the cell like a Halloween pumpkin. There was a moment's pause as the flame grew brighter, and then the explosion came. It burst through the roof of the airship in a scarlet ball, surrounded by whirling struts, girders and steel. The stern of the *Hindenburg* dropped like a falling tree.

On the ground, Herb Morrison of Radio WLS Chicago had been describing the landing for his listeners. Within a few seconds his running commentary was transformed from eager excitement to almost speechless horror as the stricken airship turned incandescent in the heat . . .

"Here it comes, ladies and gentlemen, and what a sight it is, a thrilling one, a marvellous sight . . . the sun is striking the windows of the observation deck on the westward side and sparkling like glittering jewels on the background of black velvet . . . oh . . . oh . . . oh . . . it's burst into flames . . . get out of my way, please . . . oh, my . . . this is terrible, oh, my, get out of the way, please . . . it is burning, bursting into flames and is falling . . . Oh! This is one of the worst . . . Oh! It's a terrific sight . . . Oh! . . . and all the humanity . . ."

It was 7.25, a full 35 minutes before the bomb was timed to explode.

A 400-foot flaming ball of hydrogen

ballooned from the airship. Thirty-four seconds after the main explosion, the blackened framework of the *Hindenburg* settled on the ground, like the skeleton of some monstrous prehistoric beast.

Thirteen of the passengers were killed, along with 22 of the crew. There were some astonishing escapes. Two passengers walked out of the wreckage as if it were a normal landing. Others jumped 40 feet from the observation deck and survived. One of them was Joseph Spah, performing the greatest acrobatic fall of his life. Among the dead were Captain Lehmann and Colonel Erdmann.

At the Court of Inquiry, the Americans secretly agreed not to consider the possibility of sabotage. The political implications, it was considered, were too dangerous. This suited the German representatives, who had been ordered by General Hermann Goering, Chief of the Luftwaffe, not to dig up anything that could be embarrassing to the Third Reich.

"It was an act of God," said Goering, hinting that only the Almighty could have caused the destruction of the *Hindenburg*. The committee finally settled for "St. Elmo's Fire" as among the most likely causes of the disaster, a decision which found no enthusiastic support among expert physicists but succeeded in satisfying all parties. But there *had* been a bomb. Its remains were pieced together by Detective George McCartney of the Bomb Squad of the New York Police Department.

Who placed it in Gas Cell No. IV and gave 35 people only 85 minutes longer to live? According to author Michael M. Mooney in his book *The Hindenburg*, it was one of the crew, a rigger named Eric Spehl.

### Child's play

It is a strange story. A devout Catholic with ambitions to be a priest, Spehl had slowly become disenchanted with the Nazis. His attitude hardened when his girl-friend enlisted his aid in helping a friend who had been tortured by the Gestapo. The sight so sickened Spehl that he decided to draw attention to the inhumanity of the Nazi regime by destroying its most famous symbol, the airship *Hindenburg*. It was child's play for him to place the bomb, for nobody suspected the crew.

The tragedy was that he intended the bomb to explode after the passengers had left. As it was, he was one of the victims. He was carried from the wreckage to an emergency hospital on the airfield. He was terribly burnt, but he managed to dictate a message to send to his girl-friend in Germany. It was, "I live." They were his last words. He died a few moments later. The man who took down the message was Joseph Spah.

Wide World

# THE $500,000 DROP

There are two main kinds of thief: the professional for whom crime is a way of life and the crude amateur who, for no obvious reason, suddenly embarks on an illegal escapade. Such a man was Richard Floyd McCoy. Single-handed, he hijacked a United Airlines B727, collected $500,000 ransom and left enough clues to land him straight in jail.

IT WAS easy to make two assumptions about 29-year-old Richard Floyd McCoy as he stood in the dock in Salt Lake City. In the first place he didn't look like a man with the courage or the audacity to commit the crime of which he was accused—skyjacking a jet airliner, collecting $500,000 in ransom money, and parachuting to liberty.

He was small, round-shouldered and pallid, with mousy hair already starting to thin. Secondly, if he *had* committed this act of twentieth-century piracy, it wasn't going to be easy to prove. Desoite his 29 years, McCoy was a student at the Brigham Young University in Utah. His special subject was police science. With that background you could bet he had pulled every trick he knew to cover his tracks.

Both assumptions would be wrong. McCoy, despite his diffident and unimpressive appearance, had the courage and audacity. But he was short on guile. He hadn't actually autographed the pilot's logbook, but he might just as well have done for all the chance he gave himself of escaping identification and conviction.

As everyone in the courtroom—judge, jury, counsel and members of the public—knew from watching TV and reading their newspapers, police had even found all but $30 of the $500,000 at McCoy's home in the Utah town of Provo.

## Bourbon and cigars

Parajacking, the "newest crime", was very much in the news again that Monday of June 26, 1972, when the court began choosing the jury to try McCoy. Three days earlier, a man armed with a sub-machine gun had skyjacked a Boeing 727 belonging to American Airlines on a flight from St. Louis to Tulsa; 12 hours later, having collected a ransom of $502,000, he jumped to freedom over Indiana.

It was the fifth parajacking—including the one McCoy was alleged to have pulled off—in three months, involving ransoms ranging from $200,000 upwards. Like all the others, the latest parajacking had been committed on a Friday, causing the F.B.I. to come up with a new law of criminal behaviour:

"Friday is skyjack day because it's also pay-day. Skyjackers reckon there will be plenty of money in the till, so the ransom can be rounded up quicker."

The hearing against McCoy began with what sounded like a sensation—although, in the end, it would turn out to be one of those in-things that lawyers sometimes discuss over the bourbon and cigars. The jury had not even been chosen when David Winder and Glenn Hanni, the two counsel appointed by the State because McCoy had pleaded poverty, rose to move that part of the evidence should be barred from the trial.

When the panel of potential jurors had left the courtroom, counsel explained that the evidence in question related to the finding of all but $30 of the ransom at McCoy's home. Their complaint? The search warrant said that the agent who would carry out the search had also signed the affidavit for the warrant. In fact, two separate agents had been involved.

**ALL THE EVIDENCE necessary to sew up the prosecution's case was recovered from McCoy's home. He had stored the money and his equipment in large boxes . . .**

"How are you going to get around that?" Judge Ritter asked the prosecution. James Hausley, the assistant D.A. who was prosecuting, made the point that the court was dealing with a typist's error that was of no consequence. "It is not inconsequential," said the judge. "The rule says the search warrant *shall* name the person whose affidavit has been taken in support thereof. It's a command."

### Serious mistake

After more than an hour of legal argument, the court decided that the magistrate who had issued the warrant should be recalled from his holiday in Mexico. In the meantime, the case would proceed.

The early witnesses were the aircrew. They described how Flight 855 — a United Airlines B727 — had been skyjacked shortly after take-off the previous April 7 on a flight from Denver, Colorado, to California. The skyjacker had, as it happened, almost wrecked his bid before it started — first by nearly missing the plane, then by forgetting the brown envelope containing his flight plans, typed threats, and demands. The envelope had been rushed out to the plane as it stood on the tarmac warming up.

The skyjacker, having received his envelope, retired to one of two lavatories at the rear of the aircraft. Before take-off Second Officer Kent Owen knocked on the lavatory door and asked him to take his seat in the plane. "I noticed he was wearing a wig and a big, hairy moustache," he told the court.

Air stewardess Diane Surdam then took up the story. "The plane was already taxi-ing," she said. "I told the passenger to sit down. He sat in seat 20D on the right-hand side of the rear row." The plane had only just left the ground when the passenger in 20D handed her an envelope. "Take it to the pilot," he ordered.

Inside the envelope were a pin from a hand-grenade, an empty cartridge case, typewritten threats, and the skyjacker's instructions. The plane was to land at San Francisco where he wanted a $500,000 ransom and four parachutes delivered to him.

"The crew copied down the orders,"

**PENSIVE and clearly uncertain about the future, McCoy is pictured leaving the U.S. magistrates' court after being officially charged with the hijacking . . .**

said the stewardess, "and then I returned the envelope with its contents. I told the skyjacker his instructions would be followed and to keep calm. I noticed he had a hand-grenade and a black gun with a square barrel. He made a gesture as if to indicate he was satisfied."

McCoy had already made one serious mistake by drawing attention to himself in almost missing the plane at Denver, and causing the commotion over his forgotten brown envelope. He was to make another when, at the end of a two-hour flight, the B727 landed at San Francisco. The luggage in the hold was unloaded, and he nominated one of the passengers to collect the ransom and parachutes.

With these items safely aboard, the skyjacker gave Stewardess Surdam a hand-written note ordering the other passengers to be freed and the immediate take-off of the plane, which had been refuelled for a six-hour flight.

The note said:
EVERYBODY OFF NOW EXCEPT STEWARDESSES. THEY STAY PUT. GET THE HELL OFF THE GROUND. BE QUICK ABOUT IT. USE THIS RUNWAY.

His mistake was that, unlike his other notes, he didn't get it back again once the captain had read it. He allowed the stewardess to crumple it up and put it in her purse. That error was to prove an important link in the chain of evidence against him.

The B727, trailed by two coastguard pursuit planes, took off again and headed east, following a flight plan given to the pilot, Captain Gerald Hearn, by the skyjacker. Over the township of Price the pirate ordered a south-easterly change of course that would take the plane over Lake Utah and Provo. At one point he threw out, as a decoy, two of the four parachutes, assuming, correctly, that they were bugged.

## Jaunty air

"We were near Provo when there was a whoosh sound," said Captain Hearn later. "We were at 16,000 feet and cruising at 175 m.p.h. I assumed the whoosh was the steps of the rear exit retracting again after the skyjacker jumped."

But who was the skyjacker? At the end of the first day's hearing nobody had positively identified McCoy. To Second Officer Owen he had been a man with "a wig and a big, hairy moustache". Stewardess Surdam, too, remembered the skyjacker as having "a dark black, curly wig, and bushy moustache". Could they

**BELIEVED KILLED . . . Police issued an artist's impression (right) of the Indiana hijacker, but they were astounded to discover that he was alive (above) . . .**

see him in court? Neither was prepared to say yes.

*On the second day of the trial the latest skyjacking over Indiana was still very much in the news. The newspapers were full of the fact that the $500,000 ransom had been found by a farmer in a field near Peru, Indiana. A second farmer had found the parajacker's submachine gun in another field a few miles away. The inference drawn by the police was that the parajacker himself must have died in his attempt to escape from the skyjacked aircraft.*

McCoy, unidentified by any of *his* plane's crew the previous day, looked almost over-confident as he took his place in court. His jaunty air was not to last long, however. The first witness of the day was the passenger who had collected the ransom and four parachutes at San Francisco. By a coincidence he was himself a convict, William Coggin, being returned at the time of the skyjacking to a California prison from which he had escaped—and he positively identified McCoy.

"I saw him get on the plane," he said.

"I noticed him because he was late. He was wearing sunglasses. I wondered why he was wearing them on an aircraft. He went almost at once to one of the lavatories. When he came out again his hair was not the same colour and was combed differently. His moustache was darker as well, and he had a piece of sticking plaster on his left cheek, but he was still wearing sunglasses."

Coggin agreed under cross-examination that he had seen McCoy for only 10 to 15 seconds before he disappeared into the lavatory. But he had also noticed that when McCoy reappeared in disguise "his ears made his wig stick out". It was

UPI/Quartet

26

not lost on anyone in the courtroom that McCoy had Clark Gable ears. Mrs. McCoy, a redhead, sitting in court with her six-year-old daughter, Chante, began to weep quietly to herself.

The next shock for McCoy was the evidence of Palmer Tunstall, an F.B.I. handwriting expert from Washington. He had compared the note kept by Stewardess Surdam with examples of McCoy's handwriting in government records, and with a specimen he had supplied when first questioned by the police.

### Critical time

"There are 11 or 12 similarities," said Tunstall, proceeding to give examples—the pointed top to his Ds, a double crossbar on the capital As, two different ways of writing E. The still-unresolved question of the search warrant that had been wrongly made out was beginning to look more and more academic.

*There was still no news of the missing Indiana skyjacker when the third day of McCoy's trial began. But the theory that he must have perished was backed up by a new newspaper interview with Leroy*

**F.B.I. PERSISTENCE in searching for evidence led to useful finds in the home of Martin McNally (top). But his father (above) was left to clear up their mess.**

27

*Berkebile, pilot of the Indiana jet. "I showed the parajacker an air speed indicator that was 70 m.p.h. out," he explained. "He jumped out at 320 m.p.h., not 250 m.p.h. as he thought. At that speed he would have been knocked out by the jetstream. I don't think he has any chance of having survived."*

With each passing hour of the third day of McCoy's trial it was also beginning to look as if he had no chance of surviving against the prosecution evidence piling up against him. He had been away from home at the time of the parajacking; he had been seen at the critical time near the spot where the parajacker landed; he had tried unsuccessfully earlier to involve his sister-in-law in a parajacking attempt; and, on his return home, he had boasted to the same sister-in-law that he was the man who pulled off the $500,000 coup.

McCoy landed at Springville, about six miles from his home town of Provo, and, shortly after midnight, walked into the Highspot drugstore and ordered a chocolate malt. While drinking it he wandered over to a group of teenagers and asked casually:

"Have you heard about the man who has just parachuted out of a jet west of here with $500,000 ransom?" "We started laughing," one of them told the court. "We didn't believe him. McCoy said, 'I'm serious,' and walked off." He then asked another teenager, who owned a car, to drive him to Provo for five dollars.

## Suspicions

The next witness was one of McCoy's closest friends, Robert van Ieperen, a Utah highway patrolman. "I rang McCoy when I heard the skyjacked plane was approaching Utah," he explained. "We were both National Guard pilots and civilian parachutists. Because of that we were interested in a general way in the techniques of parajacking.

"We had talked about it only a month earlier. McCoy said he thought it would

**EVEN THE COMPOST was searched at McCoy's home. The task is undertaken by an F.B.I. agent against the impressive background of the Wasatch Mountains . . .**

be possible to get away with a big sum like $500,000. I said I thought it would be necessary to use decoy parachutes to fool the spotter planes.

"I rang McCoy four times that night because I thought he would be interested to know what was going on. The last call was after midnight. He still wasn't home. At eight o'clock next morning I told an F.B.I. agent about my suspicions. I felt I had no choice."

The evidence of Mildred Burns, McCoy's unmarried sister-in-law, who had been living at his home, was even more damaging. "In February," she said, "my brother-in-law told me about a plan he had to skyjack a jet in California for $500,000, then make his escape by parachute. He said he would give me $50,000 to meet him in Nevada with a getaway car. I turned him down."

## News bulletins

McCoy, she went on, had been depressed by his lack of money. His only source of income was relief as an ex-Vietnam soldier and the money he was paid as a National Guard. "He tried to persuade me again a month later," she continued. "Then, on the night of the parajack, he arrived home some time after midnight. He looked pale and tired.

"That evening we saw a news bulletin about the parajacking on television. My brother-in-law then explained how he went into the airliner's lavatory and disguised himself after covering the keyhole with tape. He said he had asked for four parachutes so everyone would think two skyjackers were involved. He said, 'That's the one,' when a stewardess appeared on the screen. He also described how a teenager had driven him home from the Springville drugstore.

"But when I challenged him outright with being the skyjacker, he denied it. I said if I thought he had really done it I would report him to the police. He said, 'I'll kill you if you do.' Later he ordered me to leave the house."

## Double-edged sword

There was one more prosecution witness before the court turned to the disputed question of the finding of nearly all the missing ransom money in McCoy's home. Roy McDaniel, an F.B.I. fingerprint expert, testified that McCoy's fingerprints had been discovered on a magazine in the skyjacked airliner, and also on a ticket used to board the plane.

Nobody knew how McCoy had managed to smuggle the ransom money into his home unseen. The judge, however,

**THE END OF A DREAM? McCoy is led away by detectives after his arraignment. Was it merely the money he wanted? Or was he driven by a lust for adventure?**

decided—perhaps in the light of the overwhelming evidence already amassed—that evidence of its discovery should be allowed despite the error in making out the search warrant.

"McCoy's case was not prejudiced," he ruled, "because he was in the magistrate's office when the affidavit and search warrant were issued and he received copies of them. The magistrate and the D.A. should have been more careful, but the error is a constitutional point for the Appeals Court rather than a trial court."

It was felt potentially too dangerous to produce the actual $499,970 in court. Instead the jury were shown photographs of the recovered ransom. They also learned that the search had led to the discovery of a pistol, a hand-grenade and equipment—a sky-diving helmet, olive-green jump-suit and black gloves—like the ones the parajacker had worn just before baling out.

There was little the defence could do except call witnesses to the hitherto-sterling nature of McCoy's character. He was honest, opposed to violence, a former branch president of the Church of Jesus Christ of Latter-Day Saints. In the Army he had proved an excellent, and sometimes heroic, helicopter pilot. The raising of McCoy's military record proved

something of a double-edged sword. As the prosecution was quick to point out: "It merely shows that the prisoner is sufficiently daring to attempt a sky-jacking and bale out afterwards."

The jury retired at 9 p.m. and brought in a guilty verdict two hours later. While his wife wept softly, McCoy showed no emotion. In fact, he still had a bit of bounce left in him. Before sentence was passed he suggested that the judge might feel forced to bow to government pressure, clamouring for harsher sentences for skyjackers, and send him to prison for longer than he deserved.

### Escape bid

"I realize there is tremendous pressure on you because of the type of crime I was charged with," he said. "I hope you will take into consideration my past record." The plea did him no good. "The court sentences you to 45 years in a federal penitentiary," Judge Ritter announced severely.

*The news bulletins next morning announced that the Indiana parajacker had been arrested in Detroit. He was Martin McNally, a 28-year-old former petrol pump attendant. He had survived the jetstream, but it had ripped the ransom money out of his hands.*

Meantime, en route to the federal

penitentiary at Lewisburg, Pennsylvania, McCoy had already made an escape bid. During a temporary stop at Denver Jail the names of several prisoners due to appear in the State court were called out. McCoy, thinking quickly, answered to one of the names; within a few minutes he was on board a prison bus going to court. There, after feigning illness, he was allowed to go to a restroom, from which he made his escape to the street. He was recaptured, however, a couple of hundred yards away.

His plea to the judge before sentence had been prompted by his fear that he was to be treated more harshly than he deserved, and he still believes that is what happened. As he said later in a newspaper interview:

"The court made an example of me . . . If it's a long prison sentence a guy should be given the option of choosing death by execution. If I was the suicidal type, I wouldn't be here now. The only reason I'm hanging on is because I want to get back out and see my family, particularly my kids."

**"SUFFICIENTLY DARING . . ."** This was the view McCoy had of the plane as he baled out. "Only an army hero would have enough courage," argued the prosecution . . .

Picturepoint

Mary Evans

# SCARLET WOMEN

Who are the outrageous, sensual women whose lust for life carries all before them? What makes them thrive on wild passion, intrigue . . . and danger?

THE original Scarlet Woman was hardly a seductive siren. When she first makes her appearance, in the Book of Revelation, she has seven heads and 10 horns—it is not clear how the horns are distributed among the heads—and is drunk with the blood of martyrs and saints. This makes it fairly clear that what Saint John the Divine had in mind was not some Babylonian Mae West, but the city of Rome. And after the coming of Luther, Protestant theologians insisted that it was the Roman Catholic Church. It was a singularly unpromising beginning for what has become one of the great basic myths of the western world.

And it is, essentially, a modern myth. The ancient world experienced no feeling of morbid interest in the courtesan or prostitute. On the contrary, she was regarded as one of the foundation stones of a healthy society. The Babylonians took the view that every woman ought to

**WICKED THOUGHTS? This nineteenth-century photograph depicts a high-class French prostitute brooding in the rather tasteless confines of her dressing-room.**

have some experience of prostitution, so every woman in the land had to go to the temple of Venus—known as Mylitta—once in her life, and prostitute herself to a stranger.

The rule applied to everyone, from peasant girls to kings' daughters; in Phoenicia all virgins had to be ritually deflowered by a stranger before marriage. The inhabitants of Heliopolis, in Egypt, were so enraged when the Christian emperor Constantine put a stop to this custom that they burst into the temple, stripped the holy virgins naked, deflowered them, then disembowelled them, and encouraged the pigs to eat food from their stomach cavities.

In Cyprus a girl prostituted herself to

earn money for her marriage portion, and her husband took great pride in a wife who had earned him a small fortune. Early European travellers in Africa were shocked to discover that the tribal whore was regarded as an almost sacred figure. Such a girl would be bought in the slave market and ritually initiated into her trade in a public ceremony. After that, she was given a hut on the edge of the village and had to give herself to any man, youth or child who wanted her.

If she was exceptionally young or desirable there was a queue at her door for the first week or so, and she might have to satisfy a hundred men a day. Working at that pace, she inevitably lost her good looks, and then the demand dropped off. Most of these tribal prostitutes died in a very short time of venereal disease, yet they were regarded as so essential to the well-being of the community that a tribal overlord who wanted

31

this was a thoroughly unhealthy state. Society was becoming sex-obsessed, in the worst possible way. A prostitute could be ducked in a wooden cage until she was half drowned, or made to walk through the streets in a half-shift, while "respectable women" were allowed to slash and prick at her thighs. This clear division between "respectable women" and "loose women" was a product of a morbid attitude towards sex.

The Babylonians were altogether healthier when they made every woman prostitute herself once in a lifetime. This new obsession with respectability was really based on the notion that sex was a wicked activity that could only be disinfected by marriage, and that people who indulged in it without proper sanction were headed for damnation.

### Dirty books

Boccaccio had an amusing story in *The Decameron* about a randy monk who seduces an innocent girl by telling her that her vagina is Hell, and that his penis is the Devil, and that he will show her how to please God by putting the Devil in Hell. But in the seventeenth century people really believed it; a man who entered a strange vagina was headed straight for Hell. Not surprisingly, the very fact that sex was forbidden gave it an unhealthy attraction.

It is significant that there was very little pornography before the eighteenth century. There were plenty of books that were *later* considered pornographic, like *The Decameron*, *The Heptameron* by Queen Margaret of Navarre, and the *Lives*

to punish a village only had to confiscate the village whore to reduce everybody to total subjection.

The explanation, obviously, is that in primitive societies there is no *idealization* of women. They are child-bearers, beasts of burden; the male's attitude towards her is thoroughly realistic, and this is how the women expect to be treated. But as a society becomes more "civilized" a new class of woman develops. Her hands remain white, because she has servants; her body remains attractive well into middle-age, because she is not worn out with childbearing and drudgery. To a large part of the population such aristocratic ladies become remote, glamorous creatures; and the idea of romantic chivalry develops.

In Europe this happened some time around the age of King Arthur—about the 7th century A.D.; and, significantly enough, the stories of King Arthur involve one of the first of the legendary Scarlet Women, the sorceress Morgan Le Fay, King Arthur's wicked sister. She is beautiful—she never looks more than 16—and has

**PASSIONATE PHILOSOPHER ...**
**Rousseau (inset) gave his contemporaries some new ideas on love—and practised them (above). Right: Fanny Hill. ...**

had a convent education; but she studied magic under Merlin—who, in some versions, she seduces. She also tries to seduce Sir Lancelot, and generally spends her time making trouble and mischief.

These legends of King Arthur began to crystallize out around the thirteenth and fourteenth centuries. At roughly the same time Boccaccio was writing his famous—and scandalous—work *The Decameron*. In *The Decameron* the women are healthy and down-to-earth, and even Mother Superiors of convents are capable of seducing young gardeners. Yet a few centuries later *The Decameron* was a "dirty book", banned in most countries. The old, carefree sexual morality of the Middle Ages had given way to something more rigid and puritanical. "Woman" was idealized. Consequently, the prostitute was regarded with a kind of horror.

Looking back on it, we can see that

of *Gallant Ladies* by the Sieur de Bran-tôme. But real "dirty books", written for sexually frustrated people – rather than people with a sense of humour – only started to appear in the mid-eighteenth century. John Cleland's famous *Fanny Hill* was one of the first of these, and Cleland was promptly offered a pension by the government if he would promise to write no more dirty books. The "establishment" obviously felt that pornography was a real menace to the state.

Now anybody who has ever read *Fanny Hill,* which is now quite easily obtainable, will realize why it caused so much alarm. Fanny is unashamedly a Scarlet Woman. In those days women were supposed to be sternly virtuous. The most popular novel of the day was Samuel Richardson's *Clarissa,* in which the virtuous heroine is kidnapped by the wicked Lovelace and finally drugged and raped; but she refuses to yield her virtue, or even to marry the villain, and when she escapes she eventually dies for her lost honour.

On the other hand, young Fanny Hill cheerfully allows herself to be seduced – admittedly by a man she loves – then to become an older man's mistress, then starts seducing handsome young lads for the pleasure of it. . . . It was more than just pornography. It was a deliberate jeer at the current idea of female virtue. Cleland was saying: most women enjoy sex just as much as men, and if they "lose their honour" they don't commit suicide; they make the best of it.

In 1761 Jean Jacques Rousseau created an even greater scandal with a book called *The New Heloise,* in which the pretty, virtuous heroine falls in love with her handsome young tutor and yields her virginity to him because she believes that when people are truly in love sex is no longer sinful. It is difficult now to understand the universal sense of shock caused by Rousseau's dangerous thesis. Less than two centuries earlier, Shakespeare's Antony and Cleopatra hopped into bed together without causing Queen Elizabeth any concern; but now the idea of female respectability was regarded as the bedrock of society.

## Triumphant vice

It is also significant that the vilest and most sickening pornography ever written was produced in the final years of the eighteenth century by the Marquis de Sade, a French nobleman who spent most of his life in prison because of his sexual misdemeanours. De Sade is absolutely obsessed by this "virtuous" society that refuses to allow him to indulge his sexual inclinations as freely as he thinks he deserves, and the wickedest people in his works are always judges, priests and other pillars of society – who are invariably engaged in practising incest with their daughters, or raping convent girls.

De Sade wrote the ultimate attack on the idea of the virtuous woman: *Justine,* in which, from the first page onward, the chaste and innocent heroine is raped, sodomized and beaten. And at the end, just as her misfortunes seem to be over, she is struck by lightning. De Sade then followed up this tale of injured virtue with a story of triumphant vice, *Juliette.*

Juliette is Justine's sister, and she is undoubtedly the most scarlet of all scarlet women. There is no vice or wickedness that she doesn't enjoy. She even seduces her own long-lost father, and then has him murdered; and at the end of the book she is rich and happy. It is not surprising that they kept De Sade in a lunatic asylum – though his sanity was never in doubt – until he died. The "virtuous society" had produced a man who rejected everything about it, who derided all its standards, and who insisted on trying to make it see its own face in a cracked distorting mirror.

## Nausea of lust

The nineteenth century – the age of ultimate respectability – produced a nonstop flood of pornography. One of its most remarkable characters was a mystery man who is known to posterity only as "Walter". He was a "gentleman"; that is to say, he had enough money to devote most of his life to the untiring pursuit of sex.

He wrote the story of his endless sexual adventures in an astonishing document called *My Secret Life,* which is some 3000 pages long. It is instructive to compare this remarkable book with the famous *Memoirs* of Casanova, written a century earlier. Casanova also spends his life in seduction, but he regards it as one of the legitimate pleasures of life, and is interested in many other subjects – magic, philosophy and literature, for example. Walter, on the other hand, broods morbidly and single-mindedly on sex. He cannot see a woman without wondering what she is like without her clothes on, and if she is a working-class girl he always makes an effort to find out.

During the course of the book he possesses some hundreds of women, describing most of them in detail: whores, married women, virgins, even a 10-year-old girl. A phenomenon like Walter would not have been possible two centuries earlier. Men simply took sex more for granted; it was like drinking or hunting or falconry, one of the pleasures of life, not something that produced a kind of nausea of lust. The German psychologist Ivan Bloch wrote a famous *History of English Morals* in the early twentieth century, and it is mostly a description of the dozens of perversions that could be encountered in Victorian England.

BEAUTY is only one of the essential characteristics for a scarlet woman. She must also be intelligent and mysterious, like George Sand (top) and Lola Montez.

More recently Ronald Pearsall's remarkable book *The Worm in the Bud* has done the same thing. What is abundantly clear is that it was the Victorian obsession with morality and respectability that produced this explosion of morbid sexual obsession. In fact the Jack the Ripper murders were almost inevitable. The killer was undoubtedly some typical Victorian who had been brought up to think of sex as wholly sinful, and of prostitutes as an evil, degraded race. The truth, as we now know, is that most of the Ripper's victims were toothless, pathetic down-and-outs, and the only young one among them, Mary Kelly, was a strapping, boozy Irish doxy who could have knocked most men flat with a blow of her fist.

But for the average Victorian these women lived deliciously sinful lives. They even called them "daughters of joy". And the whores paid for their wicked pleasures with their horrible death at the hands of a satanic madman with a long knife. . . . Jack the Ripper, like Dracula, has become an archetypal figure of world mythology.

But even in the time of the Ripper things were changing. The puritanical sex-morality had exerted its stranglehold on European society for about two centuries, and it was time for something new. It began on the Continent, notably in France. Because of their political upheavals—the Revolution, Napoleon, the Second Empire—the French had always been less conventional than their luckier neighbours.

While Dickens, Thackeray and Trollope were writing novels for the Victorian family, Balzac and Dumas were writing about adultery and sexual intrigue, and their contemporary, George Sand—who was actually a woman—was shocking everybody by wearing men's clothes, smoking cigars and taking a succession of lovers. And in the second half of the century writers like Zola and Maupassant shocked even the French with their tales of adultery and prostitution. When an English publisher dared to issue a translation of Zola he was promptly thrown into jail.

## Over indulgence

Amazingly enough, the breath of scandal was also blowing from across the Atlantic. It was in 1855 that a thin quarto book called *Leaves of Grass* was printed in Brooklyn. The author was a journalist named Walt Whitman, and his "free verse" celebrated the vastness of America —its many people, its rivers and cities— and also the sexual pleasures of healthy men and women coupling. No one could doubt Whitman's sincerity; yet this kind of frankness was almost frightening to the respectable Victorians, who even covered

INSIDE PFAFF'S Walt Whitman is greeted by an admirer. Left: George Sand in more conventional costume. Her lovers included de Musset and Chopin.

up table legs because the very mention of legs was enough to make ladies blush.

Whitman became a storm centre of controversy. His headquarters was a beer cellar beneath Broadway, run by a German called Pfaff. "Pfaff's" became the "bohemian" rendezvous of America. Everybody who visited New York in the 1860s looked in at Pfaff's, hoping to catch a glimpse of Walt Whitman—and also of a lady who was known as the Queen of Bohemia. Her name was Ada Clare, and she was beautiful, blonde, talented—and promiscuous.

She had begun her career, in the same year as the appearance of *Leaves of Grass*, by writing rather moving little love poems, devoid of literary merit, which were published in the New York weekly *Atlas*. Ada soon had a reputation as a fine poetess, and when she started coming to Pfaff's none of the male customers objected. She wrote a regular column in the newspapers. Now at this time one of the most sought-after males in America was a handsome young pianist called Louis Gottschalk. Women swooned at his recitals. He was also a composer, whose music is now once again becoming popular—his piano pieces in syncopated rhythms are said to be the true origin of jazz.

Louis was a Don Juan—in fact his early death was due to sexual over-indulgence. As soon as Ada Clare saw him she trembled with adoration. Gottschalk was never one to pass up an opportunity, and in no time at all he had made Ada pregnant. By the time her son was born, however, Gottschalk was giving concerts and seducing women at the other end of America. But Ada did not allow the disgrace to worry her. She continued to attend Pfaff's and to take lovers.

To begin with, she was in no way dependent on literature for her income —she owned property in the south. But she lost it in the Civil War, and from then on had to make her living by her pen—and also by stage appearances. She was not a good actress, but she was persistent. People streamed to see her because she had the reputation of being beautiful and wicked. She married an actor, and apparently settled down to becoming a faithful wife; but for her fellow-countrymen she remained the Queen of Bohemia, America's own Scarlet Woman.

Ada even wrote a novel describing her love affair with Gottschalk, and with Edwin Booth, the actor-brother of Lincoln's assassin. Then, in 1874, when she was 38 a tragic accident put an end to her career—and her life. She was sitting in a chair at a dramatic agency when a small dog leapt into her lap. She continued to talk as she caressed the dog; suddenly it jumped at her face and bit her through the bridge of the nose.

The wound was not—apparently— serious or disfiguring, and it began to heal after being sterilized. But Ada was convinced the dog had rabies, and she died on March 4, 1874. The owner of the dog said it was not suffering from rabies; so it could be that Ada's death was due to fatigue and hysteria.

**PAINFULLY BEAUTIFUL, Eleonora Duse (below) excited men to frenzied passion and then left them heartbroken. She became a victim of poet D'Annunzio.**

After Ada Clare, a series of scarlet women demolished the myth that women are innocent and sexless. There was Ada Mencken, the circus rider who rode in flesh-coloured tights that made her seem naked. On one occasion friends of the poet Swinburne decided that he needed a love affair, and paid Ada £10 to seduce him; but apparently the poet was overcome with nervousness and embarrassment, and he remained a virgin. There was Lola Montez, the adventuress who caused the downfall of the Bavarian throne. There was the young French actress and novelist Colette, who not only wrote scandalously frank books but openly flaunted her lesbian love affairs.

There were actresses like Eleonora Duse and Sarah Bernhardt, whose love

**ETERNALLY MYSTERIOUS, actress Sarah Bernhardt broke almost every canon of conventional behaviour. She once took the role of Hamlet—with great success!**

affairs were known all over Europe— Duse was known to be tragically in love with the Italian poet Gabriele D'Annunzio who, in true bohemian fashion, seduced and then deserted her. There was Isadora Duncan, the dancer, who bore a child to the actor Gordon Craig, and preached a fiery gospel of free love, and who also died tragically in 1927 when her scarf caught in the wheel of a car and strangled her.

But the woman who certainly did most to shatter the Victorian ideas on demure womankind was a pretty and voluptuous young woman called Marie Stopes. Born in 1880 of highly respectable parents, she was a brilliant student of science, and decided to become a doctor. In Japan, at the age of 27, she had an unhappy and unconsummated love affair with a Japanese professor. In America, in 1911, she

Alf Mansell

**HIGHLY SENSUAL, but also a brilliant doctor, Marie Stopes (above) directed her frustrated energies into the writing of a pioneering work on sexual relations.**

met Dr. Reginald Gates and married him —then found he was impotent, and divorced him on the grounds that she was still *virgo intacta.*

Since she was a highly sensual and dominant young woman, this long frustration made her intensely unhappy, and out of this unhappiness she wrote a book called *Married Love,* which at once became a best-seller and made her famous. She married a rich man—a founder of the Avro aircraft firm—and launched a campaign for birth control. She sued Dr. Halliday Sutherland for libel when he declared that her methods were dangerous. She was finally awarded a mere £100 damages, but the case made her name known to every newspaper reader in England and America. Towards the end of her life she had the satisfaction of seeing many of her measures for birth control advocated by the Church of England—which had bitterly opposed her in earlier days—at the Lambeth Conference in 1958. She died in the same year of a cancer of the breast.

### Women's lib

We are now seeing the consequences of the work of Marie Stopes—and others like her. She may be regarded as the true founder of "Women's Lib"; she certainly did more than anyone else to bring about our modern "permissive society". It is too soon to know whether all this will produce a happier society; but it will certainly produce a less frustrated—and therefore healthier—one.

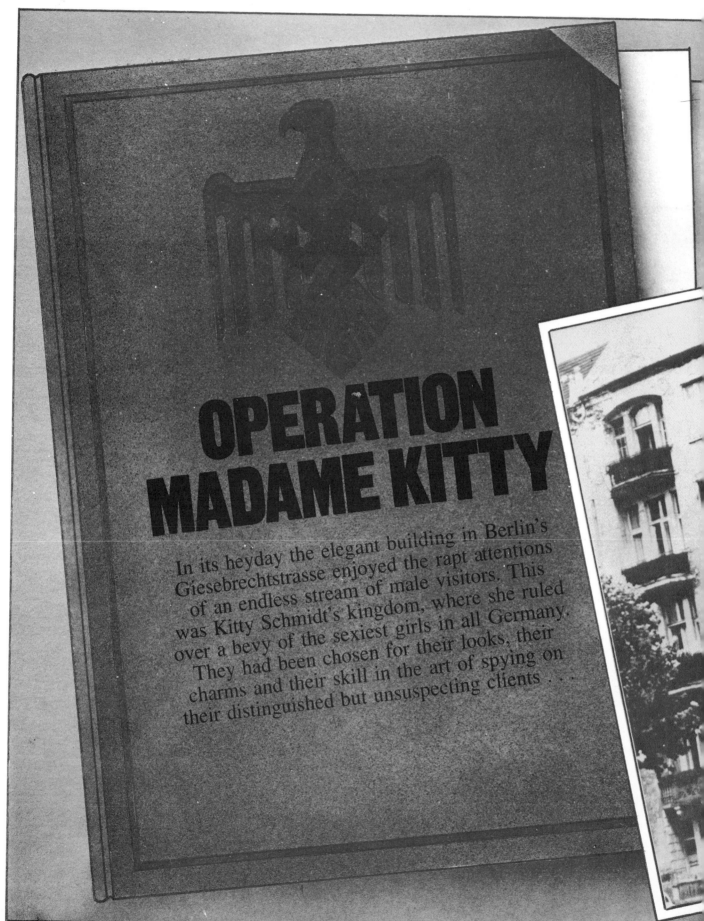

# OPERATION MADAME KITTY

In its heyday the elegant building in Berlin's Giesebrechtstrasse enjoyed the rapt attentions of an endless stream of male visitors. This was Kitty Schmidt's kingdom, where she ruled over a bevy of the sexiest girls in all Germany. They had been chosen for their looks, their charms and their skill in the art of spying on their distinguished but unsuspecting clients . . .

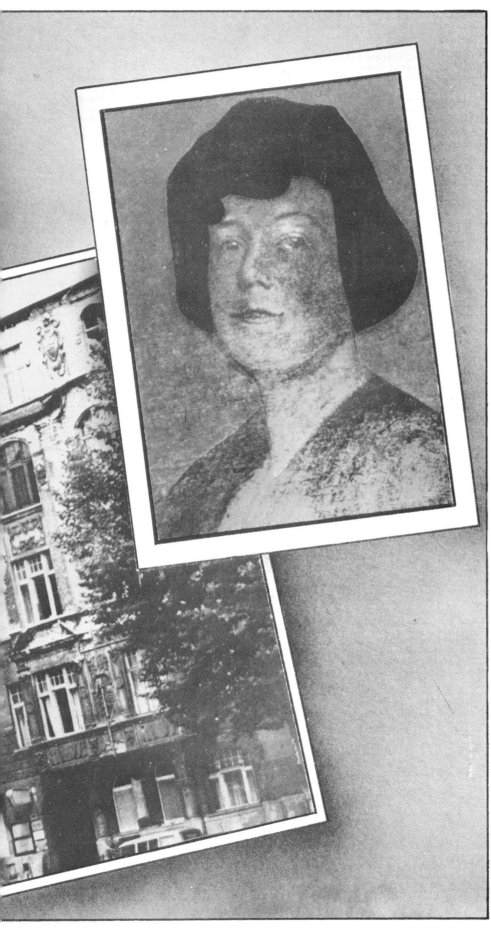

ACCORDING to city records, Kitty Schmidt owned the "Pension Schmidt", an anonymous-looking rooming-house at 11, Giesebrechtstrasse. Everyone in fashionable Berlin in the late 1930's, however, knew that the Pension was a front for the city's most luxurious and discreet brothel. At 57 Kitty was Berlin's most celebrated "Madame".

The Pension Schmidt was frequented by some of the most distinguished and influential figures in German society, by diplomats and government officials, by high-ranking officers, by famous names from the stage and movies.

They were catered for by the cream of the profession. Kitty's girls were trained to pander to every whim, to flatter, to flirt, sometimes just to listen patiently while their customers poured out their problems. Madame Kitty's fees were extremely high. What made it all worthwhile to the visitors who slipped in through the door of No. 11 was not the fine food and wines from her cellars, the expensive decor or even the all-embracing charms of the girls, but the atmosphere of absolute discretion which shrouded the establishment like the rich velvet curtains in Kitty's parlour.

### Time to go?

But, for some time, Kitty had seen the writing on the brothel wall. The rise to power of Adolf Hitler had been reflected in a subtle change in her type of clientele. Roughnecks from the Brownshirts and SS had gradually replaced her favourite Jewish bankers and industrialists. The police, who for so long had turned a benevolent eye to the Pension Schmidt — indeed, the Chief of Police was one of her most devoted customers — had begun to harass her. Somehow, Kitty felt, there was no longer any room for her individual kind of trade in the new regime.

That was why she had started to salt away her takings in Britain. By 1939 she had transferred hundreds of thousands of dollars to bank accounts in London — mainly through the aid of Jewish refugees she had helped from Berlin. On June 28 she decided it was time to slip out of Germany and join her money.

### Suave and devious

She had got as far as the frontier between Germany and Holland when a hand fell on her shoulder. Kitty spun round, to stare into the unsmiling face of a secret agent of the SD — the Sicherheitsdienst, the Nazi Central Security Organization. She had been followed from the moment she left the capital.

It took two weeks of softening-up in the cellars of the Prinz Albrechtstrasse — the Berlin headquarters of the Gestapo — before Kitty Schmidt was judged ready to meet the suave and devious head of the

SD, SS-Obersturmfuhrer Walter Schellenberg.

Schellenberg wasted no time on courtesies. "You're in trouble," he said icily. "Big trouble." He leafed through the dossier in front of him. "You realize the crimes you have committed?" Helplessly, Kitty Schmidt shook her head.

Schellenberg spread the fingers of one hand and ticked off the incriminating litany on each finger. "Helping Jews to escape—don't deny it, we have the evidence—illegally exchanging German marks for foreign currency, illegally transferring money out of the country, attempting to leave Germany without permission and travelling on a forged passport. I have no need to remind you of the penalties for such crimes?"

### Ungovernable appetites

Kitty Schmidt had read the newspapers. She knew that the punishment for at least one of the offences was death, with a living death in a concentration camp for the others. So why the lecture? Kitty's intuition told her that there was more to it than that. Schellenberg drew slowly on a cigarette. "Of course," he said, "if you can do something for me, I may be able to do something for you. Are you willing to co-operate?" Kitty knew she had no choice. "Anything, Obersturmfuhrer," she said. "Anything you say."

Kitty Schmidt was a woman of the world. She had earned her money the hard way and in her long and lurid life she thought she had heard everything. But the proposition Walter Schellenberg proceeded to make caused even her hardened jaw to sag.

In exchange for her freedom, she was virtually to hand over her brothel to the SD. There were no explanations. Schellenberg pushed an "Official Secrets" form across the desk and ordered her to sign it. The first clause read, "Any attempt to divulge Classified Information will be punishable by death." Trembling, Kitty signed. "You can now go," said Schellenberg, "but report to my office every day."

Operation "Salon Kitty" had started. Later that day, Schellenberg marched briskly into the office of Gruppenfuhrer Reinhard Heydrich—head of the entire Gestapo network—snapped "Heil Hitler!" and saluted.

Reinhard Heydrich, later to achieve infamy as "The Butcher of Prague", was one of the most frightening administrators thrown up by the Nazi Party. Ruthless, intelligent, and ambitious, he had all the warmth of an icefloe and—according to Schellenberg — "ungovernable sexual appetites". He was also a man of few words. "Well?" he said. "Everything went perfectly," replied Schellenberg. "We can now go ahead with our plans to —ah, reorganize—the Pension Schmidt."

Heydrich twisted his features into a passable imitation of a smile. "Excellent, Obersturmfuhrer!" he said. Operation Salon Kitty had been Heydrich's idea from the start. For some time the Gestapo had been concerned about careless security leaks in high places. With Germany rapidly nearing a war footing, it was essential to stem idle chatter, and—even more vital—to identify the chatterers. There was nothing like wine and beautiful women to loosen a man's tongue, Heydrich had concluded. So what better than to infiltrate an exclusive brothel and use the girls as intelligence agents, reporting back to the SD any items of value they overheard?

It was Schellenberg who had added the extra refinements. Why stop there? he had asked. Why not take over the brothel completely and use it as a vast intelligence clearing-house? Security-leak suspects, and persons under surveillance, could easily be steered unawares to the brothel. It could also be used to glean information from visiting dignitaries, foreign diplomats, and embassy staff.

There was no need to rely on Madame Kitty's girls. They could install a team of girls, specially trained in intelligence techniques, who would encourage the customers to talk freely, watching out for any indiscretions. The girls would file immediate written reports as soon as the customers left.

### Racial purity

But as a final safeguard—unknown to anyone except the highest security officials—all the rooms would be bugged, the wires leading down to a nerve-centre in the basement. Here, a team of agents working in shifts could monitor and record on disc every word uttered, confided, breathed, sighed, or exclaimed in the entire establishment. Schellenberg's electronic voyeurs could become the third ear of Nazi internal security.

Heydrich had given the go-ahead. Now the first stage in Operation Salon Kitty had been achieved. They had got their brothel. There was one monumental snag, however. They had not got the girls. That was the problem that landed on the desk of Untersturmfuhrer Karl Schwarz of the SD—the luckless agent delegated to organize the complete transformation of the Pension Schmidt.

Schwarz's first recruiting drive was a disaster. In what struck him as a brilliant stroke, he enlisted the services of the Lebensborn, the much-vaunted organization which undertook to bring together superb specimens of Aryan manhood and

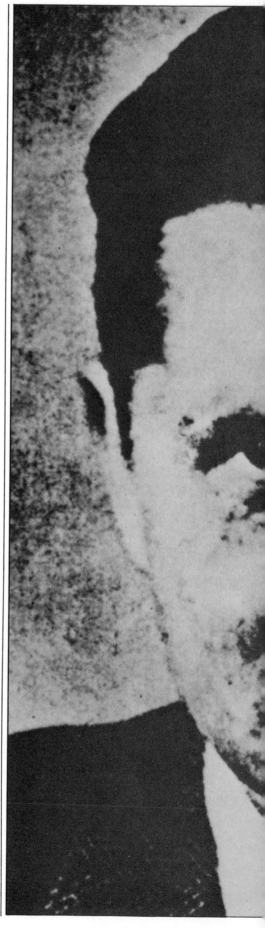

**MASTER PIMP** behind the "Salon Kitty" operation was Walter Schellenberg, who was subsequently promoted to SS Brigadefuhrer. The Allies arrested him in 1945.

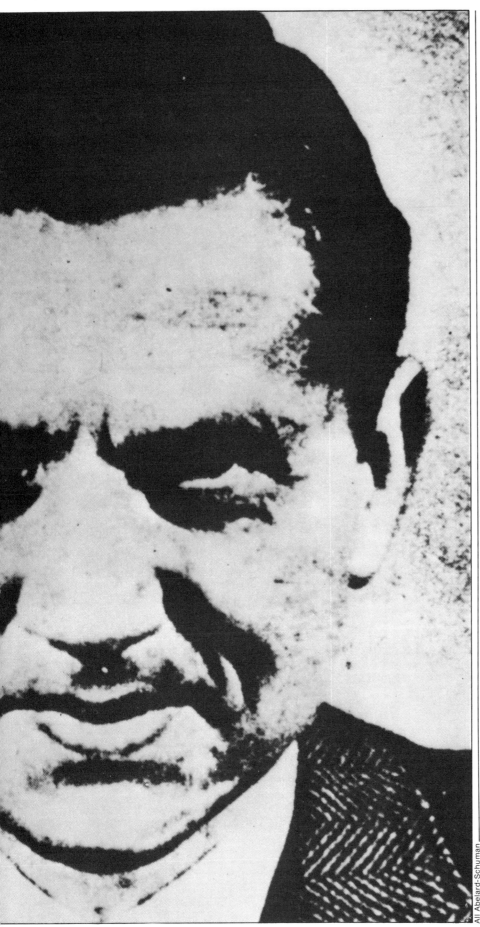

Ali Abelard-Schuman

womanhood for the purpose of breeding babies of undeniable racial purity. Schwarz's memorandum to the heads of the organization left little room for misconstruction.

"A situation has arisen," he wrote, "where we urgently need a group of women who are intelligent, attractive, have unwavering faith in the ideals of the Nazi Party and, preferably, possess a knowledge of foreign languages." The main qualification, however, was a liking for members of the opposite sex. The unspecified—but unmistakable—job would, he said, "be a wonderful opportunity for serving Fuhrer and Fatherland". There was not one reply. Breeding for the Fuhrer was one thing, soliciting was another.

## Eye-stopping agents

Undismayed, Schwarz turned to the only other alternative. Since the amateurs weren't interested, he would have to try the professionals. During the next few weeks, the Berlin vice squad carried out an unprecedented number of raids on brothels, nightclubs, "dance bars", and other known haunts of prostitutes.

Hundreds of girls were rejected outright as being "emotionally unreliable". Many others were closely questioned by teams of investigators. Eventually, the "possibles" were winnowed down to a short-list of about 90. Schwarz himself, aided by a group of psychiatrists, doctors, language consultants, and university professors, made the final selection.

The 20 girls who emerged successfully from the seven days of non-stop tests and interrogation were certainly the most eye-stopping agents ever to write their names in invisible ink. A few days later, the girls were transferred to the officers' Academy at Sonthofen—where a sealed-off wing had been set aside for their training.

For seven weeks they underwent arduous courses in foreign languages, unarmed combat, home and foreign politics, marksmanship, economics, the use of codes and ciphers, and general intelligence techniques. Experts in cookery, make-up, and hygiene gave lectures. They had to memorize posters and wall charts illustrating military uniforms and decorations. Interviewers from German radio demonstrated how conversation could be used to draw out information. There was even a grim, severe-looking woman to instil the rules of etiquette.

Meanwhile, Untersturmfuhrer Schwarz was seeing to the "redecoration" of the Pension Schmidt. The entire place was gutted. Under the pretext of renewing the electrical wiring, microphones were installed in all the bedrooms, corridors, and reception rooms—with the leads joining in a multi-core cable which ran along the guttering and down a drainpipe to the

39

listening-post in the cellar.

The cellar was completely rebuilt and bricked off, and contained five monitoring desks, each housing two record-turntables. Conversations in all seven bedrooms, Kitty's "reception" parlour, her own private room, and the kitchen could be recorded simultaneously on wax discs. On a tour of inspection, Walter Schellenberg was delighted. The place was as replete with bugs as a flophouse mattress. "I only hope," he said, "that the Salon Kitty lives up to expectations."

As it turned out, Operation Salon Kitty was to exceed their most audacious hopes. On March 25, 1940, Madame Kitty sat in the parlour of the magnificently refurbished Pension Schmidt and waited for Untersturmfuhrer Karl Schwarz to reveal the part she was expected to play in the heady new life of the brothel.

"You will be told no more than is absolutely necessary," he began. "Business will carry on as before, and you will continue to welcome all your old customers as if nothing had changed. If they enquire about the redecoration, you can explain that the place was getting a little shabby. Your existing staff of girls can stay, but there will be one small difference."

Schwarz reached into a mock-leather briefcase and pulled out a large album. It contained a selection of eyebrow-raising pictures of his 20 "horizontal agents", each girl identified by a typed list of personal details.

### Unwitting client

"Every now and again, we will direct a certain customer to your premises," he said stiffly. "Under no account will you introduce him to one of your girls. You will show him this album, and when he makes his choice you will phone for the girl in question, and she will arrive within 10 minutes. You will not discuss the client with her, and she will leave immediately the man has gone."

Kitty Schmidt knew a set-up when she saw one, but she said nothing. "How will I recognize one of your special clients?" was all she asked. "Simple," said Schwarz with a self-satisfied smirk. "He will introduce himself with the code-phrase 'I come from Rothenburg'. As soon as you hear that, you know what to do."

The time had come to test the system. The unwitting test client chosen to "launch" the Salon Kitty was Wolfgang Reichert, a young SS officer on leave in Berlin. Steering him to the salon was pimp's play. "Just say you come from Rothenburg," Schwarz winked. "I can promise you an orgy of a time." So, on April 8, 1940, Schwarz and other high-ranking SD officers listened-in gleefully to the "opening performance" in the basement monitoring-room.

At first, Reichert was a disappointment.

As the microphones followed his progress from parlour to bedroom, he babbled on about his home, his relatives, his friends in the SS, and his fervent regard for the Fuhrer. It sounded more like a recruiting advertisement than a security leak. Then the girl got to work. "I bet you want to see some real fighting soon . . ." she cooed. Reichert rose to the bait. To the horror of the eavesdroppers in the cellar, he started bragging about his unit's imminent transfer to Flensburg.

"If you ask me," he boasted, "the Fuhrer's got his eye on Sweden." "It works, it works!" cackled Schwarz, forgetting for the moment that the young officer had just let slip a vital piece of top-secret information. Salon Kitty was in business. Two hours later, the girl filed her written report, unaware that the entire conversation had already been recorded and forwarded to Gestapo headquarters, and that her talkative companion was heading for court-martial.

### Statuesque blonde

As more "Rothenburgers" were fed into the pipeline, Salon Kitty flourished as never before. Schwarz's 20 girls were soon loving round the clock. Shorter shifts were introduced as the monitoring teams slumped exhausted over their turntables. The attractions of the brothel were being increasingly touted among the country's high-ups, and Madame Kitty's guest-list read like an official reception for the Fuhrer.

When the Rothenburgers started outnumbering the genuine customers, Kitty complained that not only was the place running at a loss, she could no longer keep up with the demand for rationed food and alcohol. "Ignore the official rationing system," said Schwarz blandly. "We'll organize special supplies. As for money, put in your expenses for every Rothenburg customer."

The customers, both contrived and genuine, poured in. In 1940, nearly 10,000 people climbed up to the third floor of No. 11 Giesebrechtstrasse. At its peak, the monitoring team were recording 3000 love-session discs a month. The "stars" of the records were some of the biggest names in international diplomacy.

Sometimes the listening team got more than they bargained for. The Italian-speaking female agent who slid between the sheets with the Italian Foreign Minister, Count Galeazzo Ciano, was treated to a blistering tirade on the inadequacies of Adolf Hitler as statesman, politician, soldier, lover, and family-man. In the basement, ears patriotically burned. Count Ciano then turned to Italy's prospects in the war, and scattered an incredible amount of vital information before he remembered his reason for getting into bed. Schwarz was alerted, and a

transcript of the pillow talk was sent to Hitler. Relations between Germany and Italy were never the same again.

There was more embarrassment when the roistering, bucolic Major-General Sepp Dietrich—commander of the SS Leibstandarte, Hitler's private bodyguard—bounced into the Salon Kitty, bellowing the "Rothenburg" code-word. "Don't show me one tart," he shouted jovially as Madame Kitty flipped through the album. "Bring the lot! I want to see them on parade!"

While a maid plied Dietrich and his companions with beer, Kitty frantically phoned the number given to her by Schwarz. "Round up as many of your friends as you can," she said, "we've got a party." In the bedroom, the monitoring team were impressed by Dietrich's performance, particularly his sweeping command of sexual vocabulary, delivered in a thick Bavarian accent. But there were no dropped secrets. He fell asleep after an hour, the girl in one hand and a champagne bottle in the other.

The "Rothenburg" password only slipped up once. One evening, a soldier appeared at the door and, after some preliminary mumbles, announced "I'm from Rothenburg". He didn't look as if he would know a secret if he tripped over one, but Kitty was taking no chances. The man thumbed through the album, eyes popping like wine corks. Eventually, he settled for Isolde, a statuesque blonde twice his size, who looked as though she had just stepped out of a Wagnerian opera.

The eavesdroppers in the basement were bewildered as the man revealed to the girl while undressing that he was a private in an infantry regiment on leave from the front. One banality followed another. However hard the girl tried, the only coherent sentence she could get out of him was, "How wonderful it will be to get back to the farm after all this is over." One of the monitoring team took off his earphones. "Who on earth sent this idiot?" he demanded. Months later, the truth came out. The man was a cowhand named Krebs . . . from Rothenburg.

### Crackpot plan

Nobody was too important to be funnelled into Salon Kitty. On September 23, 1940, a telephone call warned Kitty Schmidt to be ready for a party of distinguished guests. "Make sure you pick girls who speak Spanish," said the caller. Thirty minutes later, the bell rang. Standing at the door were the German Foreign Minister, Joachim von Ribbentrop, his Spanish opposite number, Don Ramon

**FELLOW CLIENTS . . . German Foreign Minister Joachim von Ribbentrop relaxes with his Italian counterpart Count Galeazzo Ciano. Both succumbed at Kitty's.**

Serrano Suñer, and a group of Foreign Office officials. Kitty Schmidt had more important visitors than she realized, however. Down in the cellars, Walter Schellenberg himself had arrived to eavesdrop on the Foreign Minister. It was not a wasted hour. Locked in the parlour, Ribbentrop outlined a crackpot plan to Suñer involving the occupation of Gibraltar—which would have placed Germany under an impossible obligation to Spain.

Schellenberg scurried out of the building with the transcript and immediately telephoned his boss, Reinhard Heydrich. "It's monstrous!" said the Gruppen-fuhrer, secretly delighted at being handed fresh weapons to use in his long vendetta against von Ribbentrop. Heydrich reported the conversation to Heinrich Himmler, Hitler's head of the SS, who took steps to have the plan squashed instantly.

With his highly sharpened sexual tastes, it wasn't long before Heydrich yielded to desire and started visiting Salon Kitty, usually in the guise of a "tour of inspection". The inspection invariably took in several of the girls. "On these occasions," Schellenberg recalled in his *Memoirs*, "I was given special orders to turn off the listening and recording apparatus."

### British agent

It was towards the end of the year that their most unwelcome guest almost literally stumbled across the existence of Salon Kitty. Lljubo Kolchev, a junior Press secretary at the Rumanian Embassy, chose to wander down Giesebrechtstrasse at the exact moment that Untersturm-fuhrer Karl Schwarz was supervising the re-routing of the monitor-wires to a new listening post at the SD headquarters at Meineckestrasse.

Kolchev almost tripped over the wires, and Schwarz involuntarily leaned forward to steady him. Kolchev took in the whole scene in a flash: the obvious SD man in civilian clothes, the workmen who looked more like soldiers, the multi-core cable running down the drainpipe, the general air of furtive hurry. He knew Salon Kitty was on the third floor of No. 11, and the "Rothenburg" password had already been bandied about the Rumanian Embassy.

"It's an Intelligence set-up!" he thought. "A love-and-listen centre." He was well qualified to judge. For Lljubo Kolchev was in fact Roger Wilson, a British Intelligence agent operating in Berlin.

It was fortunate for Wilson that he was handsome, and something of a sexual athlete. For Control in London ordered him to keep tabs on Salon Kitty without arousing any suspicion. "We will be sending you a technician to see if there is any possibility of tapping the wires for our own use," he was told.

Kolchev, alias Wilson, became a regular visitor to the salon, keeping his eyes and ears open even at the most ecstatic moments. Eventually, his communications expert arrived. Under cover of darkness, he managed to tap two or three of the individual leads in the multi-core cable. Now the bugs had bugs, and from the end of 1940 the British Secret Service was supplied with titbits from Salon Kitty.

But the golden days of Madame Kitty's speak-your-fate machine were waning. As Allied bombing raids on Berlin became more frequent, the flood of customers dried to a nervous trickle, and the monitoring teams had little to transcribe except for ardent and climactic monosyllables. Heydrich was also using the recordings more and more as ammunition in his inter-departmental feuds at Gestapo Headquarters. In 1941, he ordered the monitoring centre to be moved to Prinz Albrecht-strasse, under his own control.

On July 17, 1942, the line from No. 11 went dead. The monitoring team tried everything, but they couldn't restore communications. Then the news was phoned in: "A bomb has just hit Kitty's." The indefatigable Untersturmfuhrer Karl Schwarz raced to the scene, his main concern being to spirit away the bugging equipment before anyone discovered it. The upper floors of No. 11 had been de-molished. Kitty Schmidt's elegant furniture, carpets, and curtains were scattered all over Giesebrechtstrasse. Schwarz threw an army cordon round the building, and ordered his men to retrieve anything in sight and store it in the cellar.

Soot-blackened and awry, Kitty Schmidt stood watching as the firemen rolled up their hoses and the soldiers left the shell of No. 11. "Report to me tomorrow," said Schwarz as he climbed into his car. With a determined lift of his chin, he added, "Salon Kitty will rise again!"

When Schwarz had a problem, everyone associated with him shared it. Before the day was out, squads of workmen

arrived to convert the relatively un-damaged ground floor into a new salon. For 48 hours they struggled non-stop. On July 19 Salon Kitty reopened for boudoir business. Even Schwarz had to admit, however, that it was no longer possible to use electronic equipment to monitor the rooms. He had to rely on written reports.

But Salon Kitty had outlived its usefulness. The Nazi hierarchy had learnt that it was one huge megaphone, eager to amplify and transmit their innermost thoughts, for or against the Fuhrer. The diplomats, the officials and the officers drifted away, leaving it to soldiers on leave and old friends of Kitty's. Discipline began to slacken among the "Rothenburg" girls, and drunken parties—strictly forbidden by Schwarz—went on far into the night, to the sound of bombs, sirens, and anti-aircraft guns.

The salon had served its purpose. In the beginning of 1943 surveillance activities were officially wound up and the premises handed back to Kitty Schmidt, now 60, fat and haggard, and looking her age. Most of the "Rothenburg" girls had come to like the place, and they agreed to carry on as her normal "staff". Before the salon was returned to her, Kitty Schmidt had to sign a second form, swearing not to divulge anything she had seen, heard, or understood of "Operation Salon Kitty". The penalty for betraying this was death.

### Extraordinary story

Within two years the Russians were at the gates of Berlin, now reduced to a wilderness of smoking rubble. The precious discs, so carefully stored in indexed filing cabinets at Gestapo headquarters, vanished. In 1954 huge crowds turned out for the funeral of Kitty Schmidt. She had honoured her word. To her dying day she never spoke about the secret of No. 11 Giesebrechtstrasse.

But the rumours about the hidden microphones, the highly trained girls, and the turntables in the cellar persisted. Only one man ever got on the right trail. For 25 years author Peter Norden investigated the extraordinary story of the love-nest-with-ears for his book, *Madam Kitty* (Abelard-Schuman). Only one thing eluded him: the whereabouts of the missing discs.

One day in 1963 he walked into a top-secret strongroom in the headquarters of the East German State Security Services in Communist East Berlin. And there they were, 25,000 of them . . . the silent graveyard of long-ago love, lust, and loose tongues.

THE PRISON CELLAR pictured was the monitoring centre for Salon Kitty. Heydrich (right) was pleased. He even managed to trap von Ribbentrop (left).

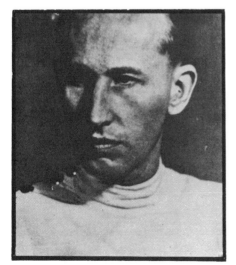

44

# THE WAR-TIME RIPPER

Night-time in London during World War II was dark and grim. But that didn't prevent the city's busy prostitutes from plying their trade. Under cover of darkness, however, another, more sinister, figure was at work—a horrifying sexual sadist!

WHEN 28-year-old Gordon Frederick Cummins, an aircraftman in the Royal Air Force, stepped into the prisoner's dock at the Old Bailey to stand trial for murder, the Crown believed it was bringing to justice a latter-day Jack the Ripper. Cummins might well have been the centre of as much publicity and notoriety as that most infamous of prostitute killers — except for one thing. This was March 1942, and blacked-out Britain was passing through one of the darkest periods of the Second World War. Attention on the home front was concentrated upon death almost nightly from German bombers.

**Throat marks**

Even so, Cummins made some headlines when his story had begun earlier that month at London's Bow Street Magistrate's Court — when he stood accused of six crimes: of the murder of Evelyn Hamilton, Evelyn Oatley, Margaret Lowe, and Doris Jouannet, and of the attempted murder of Greta Heywood and Catherine Mulcahy. To many in that courtroom he looked, at first sight, like a clean-cut young serviceman, with attractive green eyes and a fresh, boyish manner — the stuff, in fact, of which wartime heroes were made.

But the evidence showed another side to the apparently likeable young man. Detective Chief Superintendent Edward Greeno, of Scotland Yard, in charge of the murder hunt, stated that in the early hours of February 9, 1942, a woman's body had been found in the central London district of Marylebone. She had been strangled, and her silk scarf had been bound around her face, across the nose and mouth, as a gag. The body — apparently after the murder — had been dumped inside an air-raid shelter.

Greeno testified that the woman's empty handbag had been found in a nearby street, and the first indications were that she was the victim of a blackout "mugger", who had killed her when she attempted to resist him. She was identified as Miss Evelyn Margaret Hamilton, a 42-year-old qualified chemist who had recently been employed in Essex, and who was staying in London before moving on to a new job in Lincolnshire, in the north-east of England.

Only one clue, to what seemed to be an isolated murder, offered itself. It came from marks on the dead woman's throat which suggested to Chief Superintendent Fred Cherrill, of the Yard's Fingerprint Bureau, that they were made by the murderer's left hand. But the marks were bruises, and Cherrill was unable to find any fingerprints.

The following day, February 10, the body of 35-year-old Mrs. Evelyn Oatley was found in her apartment in Wardour Street, in the heart of the capital's "foreign" section, Soho. The naked corpse sprawled across a bed, as though it had been flung there, and the throat had been cut. The lower part of the body, near the sexual organs, had been ferociously slashed. By the side of the bed lay a bloodstained can-opener.

On the handle of the can-opener Cherrill had discovered faint impressions of fingerprints. He was satisfied that these had been made by a left-handed man. On a small piece of mirror, taken from the victim's handbag, he found a thumbprint, and that, he was convinced, came from a left thumb.

The court heard that Mrs. Oatley, separated from her husband, was a former showgirl who sometimes used the name of Nita Ward. She had taken to prostitution when wartime conditions had made it increasingly difficult for her to find theatre work. She had been last seen by friends on the previous evening, hailing a taxi in Piccadilly Circus in company with a young man.

The tale of death continued when — according to the police — three days later neighbours reported that they were worried about Mrs. Margaret Campbell Lowe — who appeared to be missing from her one-room flat in Gosfield Street, just off the West End's Tottenham Court Road.

Responding to the neighbours' alarm, detectives forced the door. Inside they found a room barely furnished except for a single bed, rug, and table. Near the foot of the bed lay a heap of woman's clothing, including a small pill-box-shaped hat with a feather in it. On the mantelpiece stood a glass candlestick and a half-emptied glass of beer.

Across the middle of the bed lay a "bulging" black quilt. When the quilt was stripped off detectives saw the naked body of Margaret Lowe. Around the neck was a tightly knotted silk stocking. As in the case of Evelyn Oatley, the lower part of the body had been obscenely mutilated. Scattered across the floor were a bread knife, two other knives, a poker, and a candle — all of which had been "used" on the victim.

**Fashionable hotel**

This time, Fred Cherrill testified, there was an abundance of fingerprints: on the candlestick and on the beer glass. Those on the glass were certainly of left-hand fingers and a left-hand thumb. Those on the candlestick were right-hand prints — but it was explained that a left-handed person might be expected, when removing a candle, to grasp the candle in his left hand and the candlestick in his right.

Mrs. Lowe, the court learnt, was 42, a tall, attractive woman who sometimes called herself Peggy Campbell, and who was known to many of her friends as Pearl. Before the war she had been the landlady of a boarding house in the coastal town of Southend. When the war put an end to that form of livelihood, she had drifted to London and into prostitution.

While detectives were still examining Margaret Lowe's body they received a message asking them to go immediately to Sussex Gardens, Paddington, in west London, where another dead woman had been found. This time the victim was 40-year-old Mrs. Doris Jouannet, the wife of the manager of a hotel in fashionable Sloane Square.

Mr. Jouannet said that, except on his days off, he slept each night at the hotel, and spent a few hours at home each evening with his wife. On the night of February 12 he had eaten supper with his wife at their flat; then she had walked part of the way back to the hotel with him.

"She wished me goodnight very sweetly, and her last words to me were, 'Don't be late to-morrow, darling,'" Mr. Jouannet continued. "I returned to the flat at seven o'clock on Friday night and was surprised to see that the milk had not been taken in. When I got into the flat I shouted out 'Doris', but there was no reply.

**Sadistic frenzy**

"On going into the sitting-room I found that the supper things from the night before were still on the table, and the curtains had not been drawn. I was worried, and when I found the bedroom door locked I knew something was amiss. I could not get any reply, so I went to the housekeeper and we sent for the police."

Police witnesses described the scene inside the bedroom — a scene they had advised Mr. Jouannet not to look at. Doris Jouannet's body lay across the bed, naked except for a bathrobe which had been dragged open at the front. Around her neck was a tightly knotted scarf, and, as in the other cases, the murderer had slashed at her body in a sadistic frenzy. Fingerprints were everywhere — but this time those that were identifiable belonged only to the dead woman.

But there had been another and, as it turned out, important event that same evening. It occurred when a young married woman, Greta Heywood, was in a Piccadilly bar-grill, waiting for a friend to join her for a meal. A good-looking young airman began chatting to her and eventually invited her to join him for a drink in a nearby pub.

Mrs. Heywood agreed, she said, on the understanding that it must be a "quickie" because of her appointment. They had

**HANDSOME KILLER Gordon Cummins had no difficulty in persuading women to accompany him. They were flattered by his attentions and apparent good manners.**

their drink, during which the man seemed charming and quietly pleasant. However, as they left the pub and came into the blacked-out street, the young airman suddenly said, "You must let me kiss you goodnight." He drew Mrs. Heywood into the doorway of an air-raid shelter. Then, without a word, he put his hands around her neck and began to throttle her.

In her fright she dropped the torch which, like most people in Britain, she carried to light her way. Its clatter as it fell to the sidewalk attracted the attention of a passer-by and the airman fled.

This incident, the court heard, provided the one decisive lead for which the police were seeking. When Mrs. Heywood reported the attempted attack, police officers who returned to the scene with her found that, in his frantic hurry, the assailant had dropped his service gas-mask, bearing his name and number. The name was Aircraftman Gordon Frederick Cummins.

### Totally unperturbed

Evidence was then given on the routine checks with Royal Air Force authorities which speedily led the police to Cummins' billet in St. John's Wood, in north-west London. There Cummins was questioned about the attack on Mrs. Heywood and charged with assault. His fingerprints were taken and were compared with those found on the can-opener near Mrs. Oatley's body, and the candlestick in Mrs. Lowe's room. In each case the prints matched.

Meanwhile, the prosecution stated, there had been an attack on another woman, only two hours after the attempted killing of Mrs. Heywood. In the Piccadilly area Mrs. Catherine Mulcahy met a young airman and went with him by taxi to her apartment in Southwick Street, Paddington—only a few yards from Sussex Gardens, where the murdered body of Doris Jouannet still lay awaiting discovery.

At the apartment, Mrs. Mulcahy said, the man tried to strangle her. But she reacted too quickly for him. She screamed out, kicked, and hurt him with the boots she was wearing. He ran out of the apartment so fast that he left his R.A.F. belt behind him. Mrs. Mulcahy had been able to identify Cummins.

On his arrest, the police said, Cummins had made a statement in which he claimed that on the night Miss Hamilton was murdered he and a service friend spent the evening roaming around West End bars until, at about eleven o'clock, they picked up two women. They agreed to go off with the women separately and meet again later. They did meet, Cummins said, and rolled back drunk to their billet—where some of their fellow-airmen put them to bed.

Cummins' companion was interviewed,

the magistrate was told, but produced a story with quite a different ending. He said he returned to the billet, alone, at around 6 a.m., and Cummins was then already in bed. But, the police testified, small particles of brick dust found in Cummins' gas-mask case were tested. They were found to be identical with dust samples taken from the air-raid shelter in which Miss Hamilton's body was discovered. At his billet detectives unearthed a cigarette case and fountain pen which had belonged to Margaret Lowe and Doris Jouannet.

It was on the basis of this, and other evidence, that Cummins found himself in the prisoner's dock at the Old Bailey. He seemed totally unperturbed by the accusations made against him, and stared cheerfully around the court. In accordance with the normal practice of English law he had been charged with one murder only; that of Mrs. Evelyn Oatley.

His defence was one of complete denial—even though all the evidence, first given at the magistrate's court and then repeated at the Old Bailey, pointed indisputably to him. And it was the fingerprint evidence which led to a situation unique in British criminal courts.

As a set of fingerprints was being passed to the jury for inspection, Chief Superintendent Cherrill startled everyone by

Popperfoto/Robin Clifford

**MYSTIFIED** detectives at the scene
of the murder of Evelyn Hamilton search
for clues. Cummins' identity was finally
revealed when his gas-mask was found . . .

remarking quietly to the judge: "I think, My Lord, the jury has been handed a wrong exhibit."

On the judge's direction the prints were snatched from the jury and given to the sharp-eyed Cherrill, who was waiting in the witness-box to give his evidence. Cherrill studied the exhibit and immediately confirmed his own suspicions. The prints concerned one of the other cases for which Cummins was not being tried. The judge at once asked the jury to retire while he and the lawyers for Crown and defence discussed the legal implications of the mix-up.

When the jurors were finally ushered back into the courtroom, Mr. Justice Asquith told them: "It is possible, and very probable, that, from the exhibit before you, you might have drawn certain inferences which would have made it impossible for you to try this action properly. I know I can rely on you not to mention anything that has come to your knowledge from this exhibit."

His Lordship then appealed to newspapermen to "treat this matter with every discretion", and discharged the jury. A few days later the trial was re-opened with a new jury. Once more the evidence was repeated, and once more Cummins stuck to his "I am innocent" plea.

By the time the trial reached its end it took the jury only 35 minutes to find Cummins guilty. The judge, sentencing him to death, spoke of the slaying of Mrs. Oatley as "a sexual murder of a ghoulish type". Cummins himself seemed totally unmoved. In the brief smile that he gave to those nearby there was a hint of the charm that had proved so lethal.

### Sexual escapades

Some people who knew him well, and who were in court for the verdict, recalled that he had been known as "The Count", and "The Duke", because of his educated speech and impeccable social manners. His highly respectable parents had provided him with every opportunity, but he had been a failure at school and at work. His interests were totally concentrated upon sexual escapades. The reasons for his sadism remained a mystery even to those who guarded him during his time in custody. Before his arrest no hint of his killer self had reached senior R.A.F. officers, for they had accepted him for training as a fighter pilot.

Cummins appealed against sentence, and was in relaxed and ebullient mood at the Court of Appeal as he sat between two prison officers. Several times he turned and smiled broadly at his young wife, who had stood bravely by him throughout his trial, and who was still convinced of his innocence.

But if Cummins genuinely felt that he might go free, he was to be disappointed. In dismissing the appeal, Mr. Justice Humphreys, the Lord Chief Justice, declared that "there was no scamping the evidence in this case". Superintendent Cherrill, he said, had been cross-examined in great detail, and the defence had called no witness to refute his evidence.

The Lord Chief Justice called fingerprinting "this peculiar but singularly conclusive form of evidence, because it is claimed nearly 600,000 persons have been identified without any error being known to have been made, and in no case have two people been found to have fingers or thumbs with identical marks".

Cummins was taken to Wandsworth Jail, in south London, to await execution. Despite the preoccupations of the war,

there were many who felt that the circumstances of Cummins' conviction should be further examined. The People's Common Law Society collected 10,000 signatures pleading for a stay of execution.

Chief Superintendent Greeno was asked to prepare a special report replying to points raised in the petition. But, after considering that and taking other advice, Herbert Morrison, the Home Secretary,

**THREE VICTIMS . . . Only ex-showgirl Evelyn Oatley (far left) could be said to be attractive. Evelyn Hamilton (left) and Doris Jouannet (below) were middle-aged. Why did Cummins choose them?**

Syndication International

Robin Clifford/Quartet

announced that he found no grounds for a reprieve.

Shortly before eight o'clock on the morning of June 25, 1942, Gordon Frederick Cummins—dubbed by the press "The black-out Jack the Ripper"—walked, unmoved and unrepentant, to the gallows. The noise of the falling trapdoor mingled with the distant crump of explosions as

Luftwaffe planes flew over London on a bombing raid.

The hanging of Cummins had a notable side effect on the "social" life of the capital. The thousands of prostitutes who had temporarily abandoned their operations—or confined them to well-known and trusted "regulars"—went safely back to work.

**TERROR SEIZED London's good-time girls and prostitutes as one Cummins victim followed another. The killer's success was, of course, based to a large extent on his captivating personality. Women who would otherwise not dream of accepting the overtures of a strange man seemed to be mesmerized by him. Were there so many girls who felt lonely?**

**MATCHING FRAGMENTS . . .** Thieves who broke into a store left behind them a few minute flakes of paint which had been scraped off a pair of pliers used to open a window. Keen-eyed detectives gathered the fragments which were later fitted to the pliers found at the home of the suspects (below). The Pontiac (above) belonged to girl-slayer Vollman.

# MURDER UNDER A MICROSCOPE

Every crime leaves traces of the criminal involved. But it is only in recent years that scientists have begun to perfect their methods of reading them. . . .

WHEN glass is broken, wood sawn or paint chipped, traces are left at the scene and can be transferred to the clothing of those involved. Microscopic examination and chemical analysis of such traces provide valuable information to the crime investigator.

Thus, two tiny fragments of paint found by an observant police officer at a murder scene in Edmundston, Canada, helped link the suspect to the crime. On May 13, 1958, 16-year-old vivacious Gaetane Bouchard came home after school in the afternoon and went out shopping for her mother. She did not return home.

Edmundston is a small New Brunswick town near the American border. It is the kind of place where people know each other and know what goes on. The anxious parents of the missing girl telephoned her schoolfriends, but no one seemed to have seen her since school finished that afternoon. Mr. Bouchard's questions did fill a gap in his knowledge, however—his daughter had recently been dated by John Vollman, a 20-year-old American.

### Apparent promiscuity

Vollman worked as a printer for a newspaper in Madawaska, just across the border from Edmundston. Mr. Bouchard called on Vollman's father and was told that John was on night duty at the printing plant. Undeterred, Mr. Bouchard called on the young man at his work. Vollman readily admitted having dated Gaetane several months previously but said that he was getting married within a few days to another girl.

It was getting late, about 11 p.m., when Mr. Bouchard finally informed the police that his daughter was missing from her home. A message was immediately transmitted to all mobile patrols, but Mr. Bouchard was restless—he wanted to do something. At a friend's suggestion he drove with his son to a disused gravel pit outside town which was well known to local teenagers as a lovers' retreat. With the aid of flashlights, Bouchard and his son searched the rough ground of the dark, deserted gravel pit. They found a suede slipper, instantly recognizable as Gaetane's, and not far away the girl's body lay face down in the gravel. It was cold; she was dead.

Police officers and a doctor were soon on the scene. The doctor saw that the girl was bruised about the face and had stab wounds in her chest. She had evidently been dragged over the rough ground. Several feet from the body police found a large dark patch in the gravel where blood had seeped into the ground, and close by were the imprints of a car's tyres.

Plaster casts were made of the tyre prints. In doing this, an observant police officer found two tiny chips of green paint.

One was the size of a pin head, the other was slightly larger. It was strongly suspected that the paint had been chipped off a car by stones thrown up from its wheels on the rough ground. The following day police began enquiries aimed at establishing Gaetane Bouchard's movements. They did not, at this time, know about her American boyfriend, John Vollman. Mr. Bouchard, perhaps shocked at learning of his daughter's apparent promiscuity, had not mentioned it.

It appeared that the girl had gone to a restaurant in Edmundston with two friends after school, and had bought two

**INNUMERABLE killers and thieves have been identified through the paint fragments left by their cars. Searching for such clues is part of police routine.**

chocolate bars. This was between 3.30 and 4 p.m. Gaetane then went home and quickly returned to town, where she was seen about 5 p.m. outside the same restaurant. When news of the murder spread, witnesses who had seen the girl after school on that fateful day came forward. A farmer who knew her by sight saw Gaetane and a girlfriend in the centre of town about 5 p.m. He also recalled a green Pontiac car with Maine licence plates. The driver had offered the girls a lift, which they refused. Two other witnesses also saw the green Pontiac with the Maine licence plate. But they said that Gaetane had been sitting beside the driver.

The medical report on the dead girl said that she had been stabbed nine times, once through the heart. She had not

PAINT FOUND AT ACCIDENT & PAINT FROM SUSPECT CAR

CAR  SCENE

PAINT LAYERS

been sexually assaulted. The contents of the stomach, which included some partly digested chocolate, suggested that she had died within three hours of eating the chocolate, and this put the likely time of death between 4 and 7 p.m. Some of Gaetane's school friends were questioned about the dead girl's escorts. With teenage frankness they said she had been dated by an American boy called John Vollman. Other girls had been out with him, and he had a reputation for wanting to "go too far". Enquiries confirmed that a car dealer had sold a 1952 green Pontiac to a John Vollman who lived at Madawaska.

The police decided to pay a visit to John Vollman. They told him they were making enquiries into the violent death of a girl called Gaetane Bouchard. He said that he had not seen the girl for several weeks and had been unwell during the past few days. He was asked to account for the fact that several people in Edmundston claimed to have seen him in the company of the dead girl riding in a green Pontiac. Vollman replied that they were mistaken. He added that everyone knew there were hundreds of green Pontiacs about; even the Edmundston police chief had one. This was quite true: but Vollman's car was different—it had some paint missing. The police persuaded him to hand the car over for examination. After all, if his story were true, he had nothing to lose.

**Strands of hair**

It was soon verified that Vollman's car had recently had some chips of paint knocked out of it. In particular, there was a new spot on the rocker panel under the driver's door into which one of the green paint chips found by the detectives fitted exactly. Microscopic examination of the paint surfaces confirmed this. Without doubt, then, Vollman's green Pontiac had been at the murder scene. If further corroboration were needed, strands of hair found in the dead girl's clenched fist matched Vollman's head hair.

Fragments of paint feature frequently in crime debris sent for examination to forensic laboratories. Like hair and dust, identification of paint can link a suspect to the scene of a crime. The first step is microscopic examination. The paint chip is cleanly cut through to give a cross-section. This will reveal its history layer by layer. Very often this is sufficient to indicate the type of paint to which the sample belongs—house, metal, marine or car. Under the microscope, the smallest flake of paint will take on a distinct shape and show marks and scratches which give it individuality. As in the Vollman case, it is these characteristics which enable the flake to be matched accurately with the object from which it was chipped.

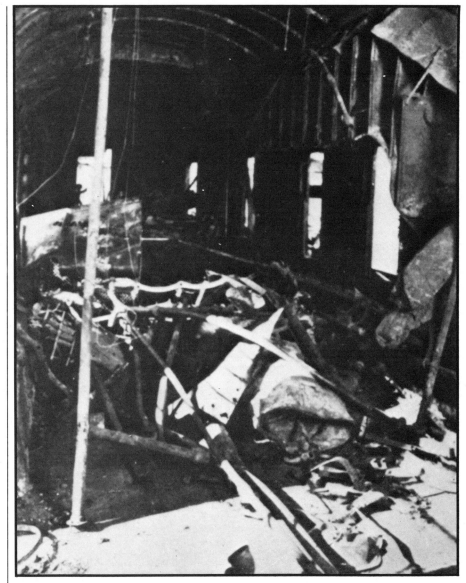

**CRIME CHEMIST Dr. Edward Heinrich (left) solved the D'Autrement brothers' train hold-up mystery by his brilliant analysis of a pair of denim overalls. . . .**

The chemical identification of paint fragments is made with a number of laboratory methods. Spectrographic analysis enables the individual constituents of paint to be identified. The scanning electron microscope incorporating X-ray analysis can identify up to 10 different elements in each of several layers in one small fragment. The laser microprobe is another highly sophisticated technique which can be used to analyze paint. A tiny part of the surface of a single layer of paint is vaporized, using an energy pulse from a laser. The vapour is then analyzed by emission spectrography which records the wavelengths produced by the elements present in the sample.

Modern forensic laboratory methods are being made increasingly sensitive, and even the smallest fragment of paint will be made to yield its secrets. The density of paint, the nature of its colour pigment and the matrix which carries it are characteristics which provide paint "fingerprints" for crime investigators. Dust and debris of various kinds have often furnished astonishing results in the hands of experienced criminologists. The skills of Dr. Edward Heinrich in this regard are almost legendary.

The famous American criminologist, after examining a pair of denim overalls discarded at the scene of a mail train robbery, compiled a virtual identikit picture of the man who had worn them. Heinrich told police that the overalls were worn by a left-handed lumberjack working with fir trees. He was aged between 21 and 25, was not more than five feet ten inches in height and weighed about 165 pounds. He had medium light hair, a fair complexion, light brown eyebrows, small hands and feet and neat personal habits. This was sufficient to tell the police that they were holding the wrong man.

On October 11, 1923, a Southern Pacific express bound for San Francisco was held up by gunmen. The train was in the Siskiyou Mountains when the engineer was told to stop the train by two gunmen who appeared from behind the engine tender. When the train slid to a halt, its line of cars was half in, half out of a tunnel. The engineer and fireman were forced at gunpoint to walk along the track towards the mail coach. At this point another robber appeared, and he placed an explosive charge under the door of the mail coach.

The explosion which followed had the undesirable effect, as far as the robbers were concerned, of setting the whole coach ablaze. They ordered the engineer to move the train out of the tunnel—he could not get the locomotive to move. The gunmen then told the brakeman to uncouple the blazing coach. Everyone was getting nervous and panicky. There was a shot, and the brakeman fell dead. Two more shots rang out, and both the engineer and fireman fell dying.

When police officers arrived on the scene they found a detonating machine and some wires and batteries. They also came across a revolver and a pair of greasy denim overalls beside the rail track. In the manhunt that ensued various characters who frequented railway property were rounded up. Among them was a garage mechanic who had grease on his clothes. An over-zealous policeman leapt to the conclusion that the grease was the same as that on the denim overalls. The man was made to put the overalls on—they fitted, and he was taken off to jail.

It was at this point that Dr. Heinrich was called in. His examination of the overalls showed that the luckless garage mechanic was not the man the police wanted. The grease on the overalls was not motor oil but fir pitch. The important discovery was of some wood dust and tiny wood chips in the right-hand pocket of the overalls. Heinrich put these under the microscope and identified them as

**FAMOUS OVERALLS . . . Heinrich's work on this apparently innocuous garment has gone down in history as a masterpiece of deduction, and made him world famous.**

**SOPHISTICATED EQUIPMENT is now needed even for routine investigations. The electron microscope (below) is one of the most important forensic tools.**

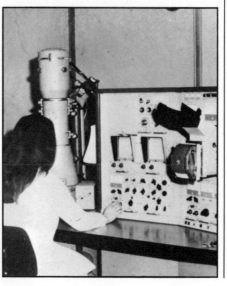

Douglas fir. The industrious criminologist also found traces of human hair, fingernail clippings and tobacco in the overalls which enabled him to devise his amazing identikit picture. But Heinrich was able to add to this description a vital piece of evidence. Deep down in the long, narrow pencil pocket of the overalls he found a registered letter receipt.

That receipt, together with the other evidence afforded by the overalls, led the police to the home of the D'Autrement brothers, twins Roy and Ray, and Hugh. They were not at home. Their father gave descriptions to the detectives —that of Roy fitted Heinrich's description of the owner of the overalls. When he was honestly employed, Roy was a lumberjack.

After three years' searching the D'Autrement brothers were apprehended and put on trial. The jury returned a verdict of guilty. The twins confessed, hoping, no doubt, for leniency, and brother Hugh followed their example; they were all given life imprisonment. Dr. Heinrich's part in this case became something of a legend. It was a triumph for scientific criminology and highlighted the importance of botanical evidence. Wood fragments, sawdust, traces of tree bark, leaves, pollens, lichens, plants and flowers form a major class of material in forensic investigation.

Botanical material, by its very nature, features in a high proportion of crimes. Leaves and bits of plants stick to the feet, pollen grains are scattered in the wind and get onto the clothing, wood that has been worked makes dust and shavings, twigs, leaves and plant fragments get into the hair and attach to the clothes—all leave traces likely to link crime and criminal.

The great value of botanical evidence is that it is often characterized geographically. Identification of pollen grains on a suspect's clothes, for example, can often be tied down to a particular district. Confronted with superior knowledge of this sort, a suspect's alibi might be broken or he might be moved to confess.

Forensic laboratories keep reference files of many of the materials such as paint, glass, wood, fibres, oils and adhesives which commonly feature in crime evidence. These enable quick identification to be made and provide important back-up information for the police. Improvements in the quality of "scene of crime" methods mean that a great deal more material finds its way to the forensic laboratory. It is important, therefore, to have analytical and reference methods to deal with it. Although there is still a place for men like Dr. Heinrich and his microscope, the modern criminologist is able to work to finer limits with ever more sophisticated methods to hand.

# IMPEACHMENT

There was a time when those who held the reins of power considered themselves above and beyond the laws of men. The way was open to corruption . . .

AS Louis the Sixteenth, King of France, stood on the scaffold, he raised his hand and shouted: "I die innocent of all the crimes I am accused of. I forgive the authors of my death, and I pray to God that the blood you are about to spill may never fall upon the head of France . . ." Many people burst into tears, and the line of soldiers guarding the scaffold suddenly wavered. A Deputy called Sancerre turned to the soldiers with drums and shouted: "Beat them, you fools, beat them!" The rattle of drums drowned the king's voice. Three executioners grabbed him and flung him across a basket, his head under the guillotine. The blade

British Museum, John Webb

THE BEGINNING . . . King John (below) signs the Magna Carta . . . and (above) the culmination: Louis XVI is guillotined.

fell instantly. The blood that gushed from the severed neck spurted several feet, drenching the front row of spectators. The crowd surged forward as the executioner held up the head by its hair; women soaked their handkerchiefs in the king's blood.

When the Marquis de Sade—the man who gave his name to the practice of sadism—heard the news, he wrote a pamphlet called "Frenchman, one more step if you wish to become Republicans!" They had executed the king; now, he said, it was time to execute God. When the French had the courage to become atheists, they would finally become free, and inaugurate a new era . . .

In a sense, de Sade was right. The death of Louis the Sixteenth *was* the end of an epoch of human history. Ever since men began to live together in tribes, the king had been the absolute ruler. He might be assassinated, or overthrown by a revolution; but while he was king, he stood above the law. Many of the kings and rulers of history practised tortures so horrible that we find it incredible that they were not murdered by their indignant subjects.

### Sheer fury

But we are forgetting that it is a part of human nature to bow down before leaders. Many ancient kings believed themselves to be gods, and some of the Roman emperors actually had themselves proclaimed gods. People didn't seem to mind if their rulers behaved badly; like the frogs in the fairy tale, they thought it right and proper that a king should destroy them if he felt like it. This attitude to kings seemed to be a basic part of human nature. And then the English started changing the course of human history.

It all started with King John, the brother of Richard the Lion Heart. John was a sadist, a tyrant and a murderer. When Richard was captured on the Third Crusade, John had himself proclaimed heir to the throne and plotted to keep his brother in captivity. John actually enjoyed being cruel. When Irish chieftains came to offer him homage, John was amused by their bushy beards and ordered them to be torn out hair by hair. He believed in making an example of his enemies, so he starved their children to death, and devised a method of crushing the old men and women under slowly increasing weights of lead.

One of his contemporaries remarked: "Hell itself would be defiled by the foul presence of King John." He was undoubtedly one of A. E. Van Vogt's "violent men", a man who lived in a kind of fantasy world in which he was god. And by 1215 his barons had had enough. John had just suffered a defeat at Poitou,

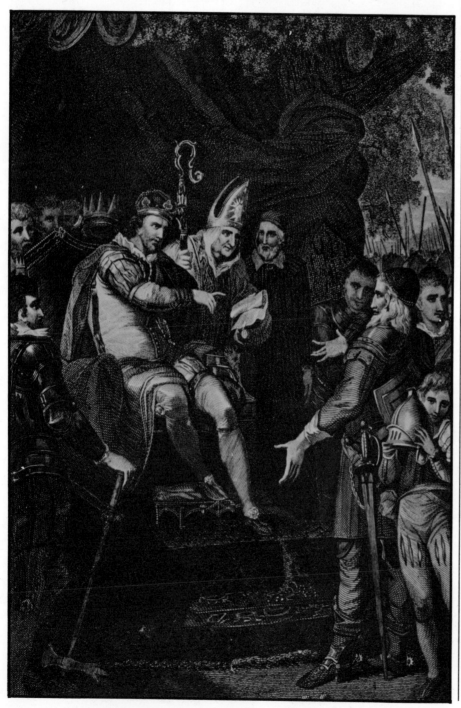

in France, and the nobles took advantage of his chastened frame of mind to tell him that, from now on, he had to rule according to the law. Naturally John's first reaction was a frenzied refusal. "They might as well ask me for my kingdom . . ."

The barons promptly mobilized; the whole country rose in arms behind them; the "violent man" crumbled; and at an island in the Thames, between Staines and Windsor, he signed Magna Carta, whose most revolutionary clause ran: "No freeman shall be seized or imprisoned . . . except by the law of the land." John loathed it with every atom of his being; something deep in his subconscious

refused to admit that he had given way and become a man like any other.

He is said to have flung himself on the floor and chewed at sticks and straw in sheer fury. At the first opportunity he repudiated the Charter, saying he had made it under duress. The whole country rose in civil war. According to the history books, John died of eating too many lampreys—a small eel—after losing his army's baggage in the Wash. The truth is that he died of rage and frustration, unable to accept his defeat. Such a man would have destroyed the earth sooner than admit that he could ever be wrong.

Having acquired a taste for freedom, the English barons went on to invent

Marv Evans

A MADMAN? The modern historian may consider such a description a little harsh for Edward III (above)—but there is no doubt that he thrived on violence.

parliamentary government, a mere 50 years after Magna Carta. But although there was a great deal of talk about justice, it was not, in fact, all that easy to get. If people had a serious complaint against someone in a high position—for example, against swindling wool merchants who used false weights—they had to address a petition to the king. And if they were very lucky, they might get justice—although it was just as likely that the king would ask the merchants for their share of the profits and let them carry on.

## Full investigation

As to the common people, they all suffered from a deadlier nuisance—war. The English kings seemed to spend all their time raising armies and fighting the Welsh, the Scots, the French and other inferior breeds. The result was military glory—and domestic ruin. The flat truth is that kings like Edward the First—"Hammer of the Scots"—and Edward the Third now strike us as madmen, shrieking with aggression and beating their chests like gorillas.

The Black Prince, son of Edward the Third, won some fine victories early in his career at Crecy and Poitiers. But the long and ruinous war with France—it went on for 100 years—finally brought England to its knees. The barons were as bad as anybody else, and finally Parliament got sick of it. The old king, Edward

Mansell

SPLENDID VICTORIES assured the popularity of the Black Prince (left) early in his career—but his constant battles wrecked the national economy.

the Third, was in his dotage and completely in the hands of a scheming mistress named Alice Perrars.

His son, the Black Prince, was sick and dying. His other son, John of Gaunt, was trying to plunder the Church to make money for the war. And the ministers and nobles were mostly crooks. The House of Commons had always taken this lying down, bowing and scraping with total servility to the king. Now, to everyone's amazement, they suddenly demanded a full investigation of the affairs of the country—and, in particular, of certain lords, who had grown rich through fraud and malpractice.

Like King John before him, John of Gaunt screamed with rage. "What are these base and ignoble knights trying to do? Do they think they're princes?" But it was no good; this time the Commons were determined. Besides, they had the support of the Black Prince, who was not fond of his younger brother, John of Gaunt. So they proceeded to impeach various lords and their associates, including Lord Latimer, the Chamberlain, Lord John Neville and Richard Lyons, a financier.

The results of this first impeachment trial were spectacular; John of Gaunt had to withdraw from the Council, and the king's sex life became a matter for open discussion. The scandals literally rocked the nation, even though there was no press or television to exploit them, and the old king was so upset by the revelations that he died in 1377; the Black Prince himself had died in the midst of all the uproar in the previous year.

## Crooks in power

Latimer and Lyons were sentenced to forfeit their property and to imprisonment, the king's mistress was banished, and nine Commons men joined the Council. For a while it looked as if the triumph of the "Good Parliament" was complete. But history wasn't yet ready for democracy. With the death of his brother and father, John of Gaunt seized power, rigged the elections to get rid of the "Good Parliament", and became the powerful adviser of the new king, Richard the Second, who was only 10 at the time. Very soon the crooks were in power again, and anyone who can remember his Shakespeare history plays from schooldays will know that England was once more plunged into war and misery.

Still, an important point had been established. Not only was the king no longer absolute ruler, but the nobles, too, had had their knuckles rapped. It was the barons who had bullied King John into signing Magna Carta, and it was the barons who had plunged England into the disastrous mess that led to the Great Impeachment. The Commons had shown they weren't afraid of the king or the barons. Admittedly the king and the barons soon regained their old ascendancy, but the idea that had inspired the Great Impeachment remained. Once it had been tasted, freedom was not easily forgotten.

## Too jealous

What impeachment meant, quite simply, was that those in power could be brought under the control of law. The rest of Europe continued to be full of little tyrants who could burn and torture their subjects at will, but in England anybody could bring a charge against the highest in the land. In 1384 a fishmonger named John Cavendish impeached the Chancellor, Michael de la Pole, for taking a bribe—£40, three yards of cloth and a large quantity of fish. Cavendish was unlucky; the Chancellor was acquitted and Cavendish was found guilty of defamation. But in no other country in the world could a fishmonger have impeached the Lord Chancellor in the first place.

Under the Tudors impeachment trials

Mary Evans

**ASSASSINATED by a fanatic, the Duke of Buckingham escaped the wrath of the people and parliament. His death was greeted with great applause everywhere . . .**

Mary Evans

**FOUND GUILTY** of high treason, the Earl of Strafford (above) is blessed by Archbishop Laud before being executed. It was a victory for parliamentary power.

stopped. Kings like Henry the Seventh and Henry the Eighth, queens like "Bloody Mary" and Queen Elizabeth, were too jealous of their power to allow anyone to share it—nobles or Commons. For more than 160 years England was back to absolute rule. The Tudors all showed immense skill in maintaining their own power.

### Homosexual favourite

But the Stuarts were a different matter. James the First was a homosexual, a neurotic and something of an exhibitionist; when his courtiers told him the crowds loved him, he said: "I'll pull down my breeches and show them my arse." His worst problem was lack of money; he had to spend a great deal of his time thinking up ingenious taxes to keep his treasury even half-full. When he finally died—of discouragement and half a dozen ailments—his successor, Charles the First, tried to solve the problem in the same way—and it finally cost him his head.

Magna Carta had been signed more than 400 years earlier; but Charles still held his naive belief in "the divine right of kings". He needed money, and he

**THE CIVIL WAR** started here, in the House of Commons, when Charles attempted to arrest John Pym with some militant friends. It meant total war.

decided to get it by every "legal" means within his power. James the First had issued a proclamation declaring that London had to stay the same size—a move that was typical of his desire to hold back the clock. Rich merchants had ignored this and built houses in the "suburbs". Charles ordered that all these houses were to be demolished—unless their owners paid a fine equivalent to three years' rent: this kind of thing made him hated throughout London.

Then he thought up another ingenious device for acquiring other people's money. He had a court called the Star Chamber, a kind of royal court that had been established by Henry the Seventh. What Charles did was to have as many crimes as possible tried in the Star Chamber—instead of the civil courts—and heavy fines imposed. It was a travesty of justice. A gentleman who had married his niece was fined £12,000. Lords who brawled at court were fined £5000 each.

But the real disaster of Charles's reign was his closest friend, the Duke of Buckingham, who had come to power as a homosexual favourite of James the First. Buckingham was an arrogant incompetent; but Charles admired him. Years previously, before Charles came to the throne, he and Buckingham had agreed that one day England should make war on Spain. Now England did, under Buckingham's generalship, and the result was a disaster; the king began an endless series of bitter squabbles with Parliament.

## Fatal mistake

When one Parliament attacked Buckingham, Charles dissolved it; a second Parliament demanded that Buckingham should be impeached; once again Charles had to dissolve it. Buckingham now led an army against the French—and once more retired, defeated. Charles decided he had to summon yet another Parliament. Once again it demanded Buckingham's impeachment, and Charles had to dissolve it yet again. It was turning into a farce. But finally, in 1628, Buckingham went to

**IRON MAN Cromwell quickly assumed the leadership when the Civil War broke out. He was a brilliant general and a highly sophisticated, if ruthless, leader.**

British Museum

Portsmouth to prepare another expedition against France, and was assassinated by a half-insane, Puritan fanatic, John Felton; the crowds in London cheered when they heard of his murder.

The king ground his teeth and swore revenge for the death of his favourite. He decided to manage without Parliament—and from 1629 until 1640 England was virtually a dictatorship. Again, the Star Chamber was used to raise cash, and then Charles made the fatal mistake of his reign; he tried to impose the English Prayer Book on the Scots, and the Scots rose up in rebellion. Charles had to recall Parliament to get money to raise an army; Parliament, enraged by 10 years of oppression and dictatorship, refused to grant it. Charles dissolved it again. But as the Scots advanced into England he had to summon Parliament once more and that was the beginning of the end.

## Illegal methods

By this time, Charles had another favourite, the Earl of Strafford, Thomas Wentworth. Wentworth had started as a violent opponent of the king, and had been imprisoned at one point for refusing to pay a "forced loan", but in the year of Buckingham's assassination he changed sides and became a king's man. Strafford was a dictator by temperament. He told Charles the things he wanted to hear: that he ought to have absolute power, and that the Parliamentary rebels ought to be "well whipped into their right senses"

In 1633 the king sent him to Ireland, and Strafford became, in effect, king of that country, brilliant and ruthless in his use of violence to raise the taxes the king needed so badly. He came back to England in 1639 as the king's principal adviser, and did his best to raise money for the war against the Scots. It was no good. Parliament hated him as much as it hated the king.

Strafford led an inadequate army against the Scots, was defeated, and had to come to terms with them. When he returned to London from that fatal expedition he knew he was probably doomed, for Parliament wanted his blood; in 1640 the Long Parliament impeached Strafford, accusing him of high treason. They said that he had tried to overthrow the fundamental laws of the kingdom, as set out in Magna Carta, and that he had been plotting to raise an Irish army to come and subdue the rebellious English—which was quite true, for Strafford would cheerfully have blown up Parliament and roasted all the rebels on spits.

In November, 1641, Strafford was thrown in the Tower of London. In court he defended himself so brilliantly that it began to look as if he might talk his way out of this tight corner, so Parliament decided to short-circuit the process of justice and bring in a "Bill of Attainder" —in effect, a judgment of total condemnation, which would deprive Strafford of all his civil rights and his property.

It was a dirty trick, as much opposed to the spirit of Magna Carta as anything Charles had done, but it worked. With the mobs of London screaming for Strafford's blood, the king gave way and signed his new favourite's death warrant; a crowd of 20,000 howled and booed as Strafford was beheaded on Tower Hill in 1641.

Parliament now proceeded to get its own back on the king for the years of dictatorship. The Star Chamber was abolished, and Charles's various methods of raising money were made illegal. After Strafford, it was the turn of Charles's other favourite, Archbishop Laud, who had caused all this trouble with his English Prayer Book; he was arrested and later beheaded.

Then Charles made a typical blunder. In spite of all his problems he was still securely the king, with half of Parliament supporting him, but in January, 1642, he marched into Parliament with a troop of soldiers and tried to arrest John Pym and various other old enemies. He was determined to get back his absolute power. It was the worst thing he could have done; Parliament could not allow the king to go chopping off the heads of members he disliked; and so the Civil War broke out. It raged for four years, with the Parliamentarians led by a man of iron, Oliver Cromwell.

After four years Charles had to concede total defeat and surrendered to the Scots. He might *still* have won through—nobody really wanted to destroy him; Parliament only wanted him to stop trying to be a dictator. But he decided to try to win back by cunning what he had lost in battle. He dragged out negotiations for so long that the Scots finally handed him over to the English.

Charles managed to escape to Carisbrooke, in the Isle of Wight, and began plotting with the Scots to get back his throne—he had to promise them to establish Presbyterianism for three years. Fighting broke out again, Oliver Cromwell defeated the Scots at Preston, and this time everybody was really sick of Charles. He had to go. In 1649 the King himself was impeached by Parliament and put on trial, accused of treason.

Anyone who learned about Charles the First by reading the story of his trial—for example, in C. V. Wedgewood's excellent book *The Trial of Charles the First*—would conclude that he was a brave, honourable, upright man who was done to death by a vicious mob of parliamentarians. He certainly put up a very fine show—perhaps the greatest and most dignified thing he ever did in his life. He refused to plead, because he said the court had no jurisdiction.

### Disgraceful trial

He declared that everything he had done in the past had been to protect the laws and liberties of England—a statement so incredible that it is amazing the court did not roar with mirth. He was told that if he refused to plead he would be regarded as guilty.

As he launched into his major speech to the court the king made an interesting slip of the tongue. He meant to say that, in reply to their accusations of illegality, he could make no particular *answer*. What he actually said was that he could make no particular charge. He obviously felt that it should have been he who was making the charges, not Parliament.

They sentenced him to death, and he accepted the sentence with dignity. On January 30, 1649, he mounted the scaffold, where two executioners in black masks awaited him. He turned to the crowd and said: "I go from a corruptible to an incorruptible crown." His old delusions of power were untouched by all he had been through.

He knelt and placed his head on the block, then stretched out his hand as a sign for the executioner to strike. The axe fell. One sharp blow did it; the king's head dropped into the basket, and a long groan burst from the crowd. They found it hard to believe that a king had actually been destroyed by the will of the people.

The blow that severed King Charles's head did not end the monarchy. The English were not really revolutionaries. A mere 11 years later another king was on the throne—Charles the Second. But no English monarch ever again had total power of life and death over his subjects. And, in effect, the trial of Charles the First was England's last impeachment. There were, in fact, others, including the disgraceful trial of Warren Hastings. But they were just an ancient survival and soon died out.

De Sade was right. It was the execution of Louis the Sixteenth of France that really inaugurated the new era of democracy. His trial was the last great impeachment in European history. It had taken the drama 600 years to run its course; the result was the freedom we now all take for granted.

THE END of an era . . . Charles I was executed on January 30, 1649, and his head placed on a spike. Above: John Pym.

# 'HIGH CRIMES AND MISDEMEANOURS...'

The U.S. Constitution provides all the necessary apparatus for impeaching the president, but only once in the history of the nation has the full legal process been enacted. The luckless victim was President Andrew Johnson whose political incompetence exposed him to the full fury of an American witch-hunt.

AFTER four bitter years the American Civil War, fought over the basic issue of freedom for Negro slaves, ended with the surrender of General Lee on April 9, 1865. Five days later, on Good Friday night, a triumphant President Lincoln took his wife and two guests to the Ford Theatre in Washington to see a performance of the comedy *Our American Cousin*. Before the night was out the President lay dying in his box, shot by an actor, John Wilkes Booth.

Next morning Andrew Johnson was sworn in as 17th President of the United

**POLITICALLY INEPT – though with a sharp mind – Johnson found himself in an ambiguous position, especially with regard to the question of Negro equality.**

States. It was an eventful start to an eventful career which would lead to his being the first U.S. President to be impeached by his government for "high crimes and misdemeanours".

Johnson was thrust into office at a critical time in American history. Politically, economically and militarily, the Southern States were in ruins. A massive task of reconstruction lay ahead. The economy had to be revived without the slave labour on which it used to depend, and a new role in society had to be found for the slaves themselves. Politically the states which had rebelled and seceded from the Union had to be reintegrated as part of a *United* States of America.

Abraham Lincoln had already promised

that reconstruction would be carried out "with malice toward none, with charity for all". As a step in this direction he had chosen Johnson as his Vice-President when running for his second term in office the previous year.

Lincoln was a Republican, his Vice-President a Democrat. At the outbreak of the war Johnson had, in fact, been a senator for Tennessee, one of the Southern States, but he had remained loyal to the Union throughout the struggle. Lincoln's motive in appointing a political opponent as a running mate had been that, with the end of the war clearly in sight, he wanted to offer the largely Democratic South a token of goodwill.

The man who now found himself unexpectedly in charge of the peace had a

massive head, luxurious dark hair, piercing eyes, a strong chin, and a cold, reserved nature, the result of his early struggles. He had been born 56 years earlier at Raleigh, North Carolina, where he was apprenticed to a tailor at the age of 10. At 18, after moving to Tennessee, he married 16-year-old Eliza McCardle, who had a fair education and taught him reading, writing and arithmetic. Johnson, in fact, does not only enjoy the distinction of being the only U.S. President impeached by his government; he is also the only U.S. President who never went to school.

### Slaveowner

Nevertheless, he had worked his way up the political ladder after being elected mayor of Greeneville, Tennessee, at the age of 21. The rough-and-tumble of southern politics remained his forte, however. As President he showed an appalling lack of political sophistication.

The cards were, of course, stacked against him. He was a Southerner leading Northerners. He was a Democrat while both Congress and the Senate were strongly Republican, mostly favouring a tough radical line towards the defeated Confederates. He was an ex-slaveowner presiding over the dissolution of slavery. If he had been more politically astute, he might have overcome these difficulties. He never seemed to grasp, however, that he had no genuine political following in Washington, and could not hope to act without marshalling political and public opinion behind him.

### Whole person

It is therefore hardly surprising that he was on a collision course with Congress and the Senate practically from the moment he took office. One of his first steps, in May 1865, was to grant an amnesty to millions of rebels and leave their former leaders free to organize new State governments, subject to such steps as rescinding secession from the Union and abolishing slavery.

The decision caused uproar among the radical Republicans. The President, they complained, had acted while both houses were in holiday recess. No provision had been made for two moves dear to Republican hearts because they would break the Democrat stranglehold on the South—disfranchising a large number of white rebels and giving the vote to Negroes, who would presumably support their Republican liberators. Furthermore, with Washington still seething over stories of rebel atrocities, the Republicans believed no white Southerner should be allowed to hold political office unless he and his State had proved their loyalty.

From the Republican point of view the question of rigging the voting against the Southern Democrats was particularly critical. In the past the number of delegates to Washington from the 11 rebel States had been arrived at on a population basis, with each slave counting as "three-fifths of a human being". Now, under the 13th Amendment to the Constitution which had abolished slavery, each ex-slave—and there were four million of them—would count as a whole person. That meant a substantial increase in Southern delegates, perhaps as many as 40, who, unless something was done,

**A GREAT AMERICAN lies on his death-bed. Lincoln's assassination immediately brought Johnson (ringed) to power and destroyed the delicate political balance.**

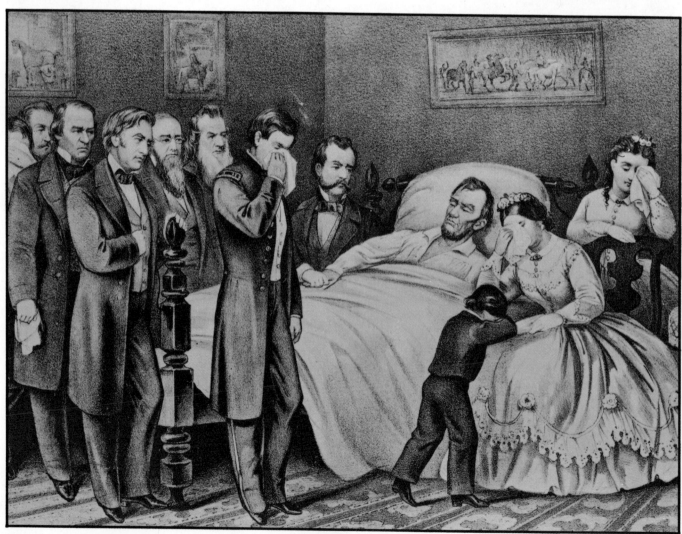

Bettmann

would be Democratic delegates. The Republicans feared they would lose in the debating chamber the war they had just won on the battlefield.

However, they found Johnson "harsh, petulant and unreasonable" when they protested to him. One radical Republican senator, Charles Sumner, complained that Johnson attacked him with cheap analogies in answer to his argument that the South was torn by racial violence and not ready for admission to the Union.

### Immediate votes

"Are there no murders in Massachusetts?" Johnson asked. "Unfortunately, yes," replied Sumner. "Would you consent on this account that Massachusetts should be excluded from the Union?" Johnson asked triumphantly, at the same time spitting absentmindedly into Sumner's top hat, which he had placed upside down on the floor.

Congress responded when it met in December by refusing admission to the newly chosen rebel representatives who were former Confederate leaders practically to a man and, in most cases, had worn the grey uniform of the South. Congress and the Senate set up their own joint committee on reconstruction. They also demanded immediate votes for Negroes and disfranchisement of a large number of white rebels. Johnson refused both demands.

### Open hostility

As a result the Southern States remained without a voice in Washington while the joint committee investigated their loyalty, eventually reporting in June 1866 that they were unfit for representation. That same month Congress passed a 14th Amendment to the Constitution, laying down the principle of racial equality.

Any state which deprived any male citizen over 21 of the right to vote would be penalized. The amendment also stipulated that citizens "guilty of participation in rebellion" could be denied the vote. Confederates who had held office before the war were barred from holding state or federal office without the approval of

**SOUTHERN REBELS were officially pardoned by Johnson (left). The result: Republican anger. Then he sacked Stanton (top), who quickly became a scapegoat . . .**

two-thirds of each house of Congress.

To become law the amendment had to be ratified by three-quarters of the States. Johnson advised the Southern States to reject it. All of them did so but one: his own State of Tennessee. A climate of open hostility now existed between the President and Congress. Johnson went on record as saying the Negro was too ignorant to vote. He also used his power of veto to obstruct a number of liberal reconstruction bills. It is said, in fact, that he vetoed more bills than all the previous 16 Presidents put together.

Against this background the mid-term Congressional elections took place in November 1866. It was a rough campaign with the Republicans determined to establish a two-thirds majority which would enable them to re-pass bills over the Presidential veto.

Johnson tried to form a third party, a

Bettmann

**"YOU ARE SUMMONED to appear before the Senate . . ."** George T. Brown, Sergeant-at-Arms of the Senate, delivers the official impeachment papers to Johnson.

still in the field." He also attacked the standing of Congress.

His opponents were quick to pounce on his words and denounce him as "a trickster, touched by insanity, corrupted with lust, stimulated by drink". The Republicans were able to point out with justification that, although the Southern States had lost the battle over Negro slavery, the provisional governments set up by the President had brought in Black Codes designed to keep Negroes in a state of subjection.

### Vengeance

Alabama, for instance, had made provision that "any stubborn or refractory servants" or "servants who loiter away their time" should be fined 50 dollars. It was clear, the Republicans argued, that, with the connivance and support of the President, the rebel States had no intention of protecting Negroes' basic rights. The truth of the argument seemed borne out by bitter race riots in Memphis and New Orleans, resulting in 40 deaths, most of the victims being Negroes.

The result of the elections was a Republican triumph. They easily achieved the two-thirds majority needed to overturn the Presidential veto, and they set about the task of reconstruction with, quite literally, a vengeance. The Reconstruction Act of March 1867 divided the South into five military districts. Each had a federal garrison under a general whose first task was to set up new State governments in place of those created by the President.

The act also defined the process of re-admission to the Union. Each State had to frame and approve a constitution which included Negro franchise. Each State had also to ratify the 14th Amendment. Once the State constitution had been approved by Congress, the State itself automatically gained the right to be represented again in Washington.

### Dubious means

The effect of the new legislation was to disfranchise a large section of the traditional Democratic vote and create a predominantly pro-Republican electorate in which Negroes outnumbered the whites, and, of those whites, the great majority were either "scalawags"—Southerners willing to co-operate with the Radicals—or "carpetbaggers"—Northerners who had moved South since the war for a variety of reasons, but usually the desire to get rich quick by dubious means.

With that achieved, the Radicals turned their attention to the actual Presidency and made a totally unconstitutional,

coalition of white Southerners, Democrats from the North, moderate Republicans and Presidential appointees. The party did not catch on with the electorate because it had no grass-roots support. And Johnson also damaged his cause by the chronic lack of discretion with which he was inflicted.

### No drunkard

This had been demonstrated at his inauguration, when he got drunk and treated his audience to a long harangue about the poverty of his youth and his hard-won success. His supporters pleaded that he had taken only three glasses of whisky, which had affected him because he was weak after a severe attack of typhoid fever. Lincoln, too, leaped to his defence,

explaining, "I have known Andy for many years. He made a bad slip the other day, but he ain't no drunkard." It wasn't, however, an incident his political opponents were about to let anyone forget.

Now, in "a swing around the circle" to drum up electoral support, he made a number of reckless speeches. In one he accused two leading Republicans, one in Congress, one in the Senate, of complicity in the assassination of Lincoln—a charge which had also been levelled at him.

In another, referring to his loyalty to the Union throughout the war, he thundered, "I fought traitors and treason in the South. Now, when I turn round at the other end of the line and find men who will stand opposed to the union of these States, I am free to say to you that I am

direct attack on Johnson's traditional powers. The President's position as Commander-in-Chief was assaulted by another act of March 1867 which placed the major-generals under General Grant, victor in the Civil War and commanding general of the army. Further, the act stipulated that Grant could not be removed from his command or sent away from Washington.

### Implacable enemy

The final insult was the Tenure of Office Act, passed in the same month, which barred the President from dismissing any office-holder without the approval of the Senate. This denied Johnson the right to control his own cabinet, thus threatening a precedent going back to the time of Washington, and left him with no more than a minor, passive role in legislation.

Johnson responded by sacking Edwin Stanton, his Secretary of War. It is a mystery why he waited so long. Stanton, whom he had inherited from Lincoln, was —as the President knew—a shifty, implacable enemy who had long intrigued against him. Even today a considerable

THESE MEN (left) were the duly appointed managers of the impeachment trial. Below: the Senate in full flow against the nation's chief executive.

Nigel Morland, Bettmann/Quartet

679

**HIGH-MINDED? Perhaps. But Benjamin Butler (above), who led the prosecution case against Johnson (left), could also be accused of self-righteous bombast ...**

amount of circumstantial evidence exists to link Stanton with the "Lincoln assassination" plot; his name was frequently mentioned in connection with it during Johnson's years of office. Yet, although aware he was nurturing an enemy, and possibly an assassin, in his cabinet, the President, strangely, did nothing about removing him until he knew it would precipitate another head-on collision with Congress and the Senate.

### High crimes

What was to be a two-day debate on the President's action began on February 24, 1868. It ended with another victory on February 26 for the anti-Johnson forces. It was resolved by 126 votes to 47 "that Andrew Johnson, President of the United States, be impeached for high crimes and misdemeanours in office".

The protracted proceedings began on March 5, 1868, with the formal statement of the charges before the 54 members of the Senate serving as a "jury" to decide the issue. The accusation was that Johnson had attempted to remove Stanton. It was also alleged that, during his "swing around the circle" speeches, he tried to "bring into disgrace, ridicule, contempt and reproach the Congress of the United States" by claiming its legislation was invalid because the elected rebel leaders had been barred from taking their seats.

### Tyrannical imbecile

He was also accused of being "unmindful" of the high duties of his office and "of the harmony and courtesies which ought to exist between the executive and legislative branches of the government".

Johnson made his formal reply to the charges on March 23. He claimed the right, as President, to dismiss his Secretary for War, pointing out that, in any case, Stanton had been Lincoln's appointment, not his. He denied he had attacked the validity of the legislation passed by Congress, but, even if he had, he believed the right to free speech entitled him to state his opinions. The President did not appear in person, he sent attorneys with his reply.

The proceedings warmed up on March 30 with the opening speech for the "prosecution", made by Benjamin F. Butler of Massachusetts, one of the leading radical Republicans. The Senate was packed solid on that blowy, sunny day, with the senators ranged in a great series of semicircles before the Speaker and Chief Justice and not a seat free in the Press and public galleries.

Butler adopted a lofty tone. He began by congratulating the United States on having created machinery for impeaching and sacking Presidents in contrast to other countries who "have found no mode by which to rid themselves of a tyrannical, imbecile or faithless ruler save by overturning the very foundation and framework of the government itself".

He attacked the attempt to remove Stanton, going so far as to say that the issue at stake was "whether the Presidential office, if it bears the prerogatives and powers claimed for it, ought, in fact, to exist as a part of the constitutional government of a free people".

He also denied the right of the President to "speak what he pleases in what manner he pleases". As President he should be more circumspect than the private citizen. Instead, Johnson had exposed "to the taunts and ridicule of every nation the good name and fame of the chosen institutions of thirty million people".

"Never again, if Andrew Johnson go quit and free this day," he warned extravagantly, "can the people of this or any other country by constitutional checks or guards stay the usurpation of executive power . . . the political welfare and liberties of all men hang trembling on the decision of this hour."

### Purely political

"This hour" stretched into weeks, with ever more witnesses, more oratory. One of the major issues was what Johnson had or hadn't said in his election speeches. In Cleveland, for instance, had he uttered the words: "We have seen this Congress assume, or pretend to be, for the Union . . ."?

Copies of the *Cleveland Dealer,* a newspaper known to be hostile to Johnson, were produced. They contained the words. Neither the editor nor the reporter who had covered the story together were able, however, to produce their original notes. "I don't know where they are," said the editor, adding that, like some of the Watergate evidence more than a century later, they had "probably been destroyed".

By the time the 54 senators got around to voting on the issues on May 26, it had become quite clear that the impeachment proceedings had no real substance, but were a purely political attack by the Republicans on the President.

### Naturally sterile

That attack failed in the end by the narrowest of margins, merely because a number of Republican senators voted for their conscience rather than their party. The final vote was 35-19 against the President. It was, however, one vote short of the two-thirds majority needed to remove him from office.

The remaining six months of Johnson's reign as President were naturally sterile. Then he was ousted from office and replaced by the Republican General Grant, the Eisenhower of his time. It was, however, only the rigged vote in the Southern States, where Negroes had been enfranchised and white rebels barred from the ballot box, that gave the Republicans victory. The final figures were 3,012,883 for Grant, 2,703,249 against.

For the Northern Republicans this narrow success underlined the importance of continuing to hold down the Southern white Democrats and, by any means, to win the Negro vote.

Nigel Morland, Culver

The result was to make the disfranchised Southerners turn to their most radical leaders. It led as well to the founding of the Ku Klux Klan, partly to protect terrorized whites, partly as a reprisal force. Carpetbaggers were whipped, tarred and feathered. Superstitious Negroes were driven from the polling booth by ghostly white figures rattling skulls.

### Brilliant speech

But the white Southerners could not be held down for ever. With the passing of the years, historic hatreds waned, and in Washington the old guard of hard-line Republicans gradually died or retired. The question began to be asked: Is it worth spending public money to force the South to treat the Negro as a first-class citizen when most of the North treats him as a second-class citizen?

Gradually white Southerners got the

**SAVED BY DOUBT . . . One vote came between Johnson and conviction. Six months after the verdict, his term ended and Yankee General Grant replaced him.**

vote back, and in 1874 the Democrats won the Congressional elections. Johnson, after several unsuccessful attempts, was returned to the Senate for Tennessee again the following year. He made one last brilliant speech, defending his own reconstruction policy and roundly condemning that of the Republicans, then he died.

Of his policy it can be said that he genuinely believed the liberated Negro would have to be turned into a first-class citizen by degrees rather than by a single stroke of the pen. In effect, however, he made the Negro a political pawn and sowed the seeds of the Civil Rights controversy which is still a disruptive force in the United States today.

WHEN Warren Hastings reflected upon the happenings and trial that led him from being one of the most influential men in the rising British Empire to one of its most dishonoured public servants, he probably traced the whole amazing chapter of events back to one isolated, and apparently unconnected, incident.

It happened on a summer's day in 1780 when Hastings, Britain's first Governor-General of India, was conducting a meeting of his ruling Council of five. Suddenly the colour heightened in his face; he pushed back his chair, picked up his glove and threw it violently upon the table.

The glove landed in front of Sir Philip Francis, a Council member. In that single, expressive gesture Hastings was challenging his colleague to a duel—the result of which was to be burned upon his memory for ever after.

From the moment the two Englishmen met in India the venomous Sir Philip **IRRATIONAL HATRED seemed to lie behind the vendetta conducted by Francis (right). The press sided with Hastings even in cartoons (below right) whilst Burke (bottom) was satirized. Exclusive trial invitations (below) were printed.**

had taken a dislike to Hastings. At every meeting of the Council he goaded and opposed the mild-mannered Governor-General; on every occasion he slandered and libelled Hastings.

Faced with such violent opposition, there was little that the Governor-General could do. He ruled for both the mighty East India Co pany and the British Government, which supported the Company financially—an imperfect alliance of employers. His system of administration was laid down by the British Government, and from it Hastings had to satisfy the Company's shareholders, the Government's taxpayers, and feuding native rulers in India—who owed at least a nominal allegiance not to the British Empire but to the Empire of the Grand Mogul.

Hastings was implacably opposed by Francis, who, gaining the support of the other three members of the Council, kept the Governor-General in a permanent minority. Together, they did their utmost to undo Hastings' reforms. They cancelled a treaty he had necessarily made with a native ruler, and even put him "on trial"

# AN OLD COLONIAL SCORE

The Governor-General of India Warren Hastings was, by most standards, a highly able administrator and he presided over the ruling Council with firmness and discretion. Unfortunately he ran foul of the formidable Sir Philip Francis a Council member of violent temper and venomous spite . . .

in his own Council room.

For years Hastings opposed his detractors within the constraints forced upon him by the administrative rules. Sent to Bengal to rid the East India Company of wholesale corruption, and to administer justice to the territory, he found the Company's affairs in chaos. And "private trading", openly practised by the Company's officials, often amounted to defrauding the local natives.

In the field of Indian foreign affairs Hastings had to contend with marauders from Afghanistan and lawless Indians who frequently attacked Bengal; French spies encouraging the native population to revolt; and the French navy sailing to attack the colony's coastline.

When the arrogant Sir Philip Francis added his domestic harassment to all these problems Hastings' patience broke. Dramatically, he threw down his glove. He wanted a duel, nothing less.

Several days later the two combatants met in a field in Calcutta at six o'clock in the morning. They stood back to back; then began to walk. As their seconds called to them to turn, pistols cracked.

## A duel

Sir Philip misfired, but Hastings' bullet went straight into his opponent's chest. Bleeding and badly wounded, he was carried from the field. Unfortunately for Hastings, Sir Philip lived, and as soon as he was able, he set sail for England to gain his revenge on the Governor-General. Meanwhile, in London, the venomous Francis found the ear of the fiery Irish politician Edmund Burke.

Burke was one of those key reformers whom no Radical party, whatever the age, seems to be without. They leave their mark for their zeal in believing that the protection of the poor, the afflicted, and the underdog is all that matters in life. While the sentiment is a noble one, sometimes it is prey to the argument: who in fact are the underdogs, and who is the oppressor?

Edmund Burke never gave a thought to that argument when the story of Warren Hastings, as told by Sir Philip Francis, was unfolded to him. His chest swelled with rage and indignation. Here was an outrageous case of an omnipotent public servant grinding down the natives of a far-off land; the very same people who, in their helplessness, should have been defended by the mother country.

Furiously, Burke harangued the House of Commons. If nothing were done about the villainous Hastings he would resign his minor Ministry of Paymaster of the

**WHAT MOTIVE lay behind the uncompromising attitude of Sir Philip Francis? Did he secretly covet the power and influence wielded by his enemy?**

Forces. At first the Commons were lukewarm; then Burke gained some Radical allies. Even so, it took him five years of oratory, from 1782 to 1787, before Parliament would agree to Hastings' impeachment, and in that time Hastings had already retired from his Governor-Generalship.

## Indian politics

He had been received by King George the Third with distinction upon his return to England. The directors of the East India Company also gratefully acknowledged their debt to him by a unanimous vote of thanks. Only Burke, spurred by the scurrilous tales of Francis, went blindly on and succeeded in swaying a Parliament that had become suddenly conscious of its new liberal spirit.

For someone like Francis, the task of twisting the facts presented few problems, for it was all too easy to put a wrong construction upon almost everything Hastings had done in India. The Governor-General's first important policy had been to arrange a treaty with the Nawab of Oudh, with a view to using Oudh as a bulwark against the rebellious Mahrattas. In exchange, the Nawab wanted English troops to help him overcome the Rohillas

tribe. Hastings complied, and the Nawab's victory was followed by more than the usual atrocities by his troops.

When a local chief, Nuncomar, offered himself as a candidate for the post of Deputy Ruler of Bengal, Hastings preferred another. Nuncomar, piqued by his failure, declared that the Governor-General had taken bribes. Not long afterwards Nuncomar himself was arrested and tried for conspiracy and forgery and, in the spirit of those times, having been found guilty, he was hanged.

During the time when the American War of Independence was claiming total British attention, Hastings became embroiled in a desperate battle to save India for the British. The principal enemy was Hyder Ali, ruler of Mysore, whose troops swept over the Carnatic and defeated the British Army. Hastings then directed all his forces against Hyder Ali, and, despite the arrival of French troops as allies to Mysore, the ruler was defeated.

## Bribery or tribute?

Because wars have to be paid for, and because it was the East India Company's custom to exact tribute from the local rulers, Hastings had asked the Rajah of Benares — as a dependant of the Company

Mary Evans

—for a contribution. When the Rajah refused, Hastings was obliged to join battle and, after the victory, to depose him.

Next, Hastings had asked the new ruler of Oudh for his contribution. A two-sided power split in that territory made collection difficult; in the mix-up, it was clear that one side paid and the other didn't, and that the side that did pay tried to exact the other side's share by torture.

It was clear, too, that although Hastings was taking large sums of money as presents, he was paying them immediately into the Company's funds in lieu of tribute—simply because it seemed an easier way of collecting taxes from reluctant payers.

### Impeachment

All these facts were given a new edge, a sinister twist, by the malicious Philip Francis, causing his ready listener, Burke, to denounce Hastings in the Commons as "the grand delinquent of all India". The turning point against Hastings came when, for some reason which has never been satisfactorily explained, the younger Pitt, who was Prime Minister, suddenly changed his attitude from that of an ally of Hastings to that of a foe. On May 10, 1787, the Commons took the step for

which Burke and Francis had so fervently worked—a vote for impeachment.

The prosecution of the impeachment articles, it was decided, would be in the hands of "managers". Those chosen to lead these managers were a Radical trio —Burke, his Commons ally Charles James Fox, and Richard Brinsley Sheridan, theatre manager, playwright, author of *The School for Scandal* and *The Rivals*, and something for an exhibitionist M.P.

That none of these managers or their leaders was a trained lawyer, aware even of the rules of relevance and admissibility, was in due course to prove an embarrassing and highly expensive oversight. On February 13, 1788, the trial opened in Westminster Hall. It began with a procession of 170 peers from the House of Lords, dressed in their gold and ermine— among them the brothers and sons of the King; the Prince of Wales, "conspicuous by his fine person and noble bearing"; the Queen; and by her side "the fair-haired daughters of the House of Brunswick".

After those in the procession had taken their places, Burke entered the Hall. A woman spectator later described his entry in a letter: "He held a scroll in his hand, and walked alone, his brow knit with corroding care and labouring thought."

**THE OPENING DAY of the trial saw a courtroom packed with eager spectators. Six years later there were only a few ageing peers left to vote on a verdict.**

They watched, these celebrities, with riveted attention as Hastings, a little man "dressed in a plain poppy-coloured suit of clothes" surrendered, kneeling before the Lord Chancellor, Lord Thurlow. No one thought he looked like a man who for 13 years had ruled an entire sub-continent. According to one account:

### Seven year trial

"He looked like a great man, and not like a bad man. A person small and emaciated, yet deriving dignity from a carriage which indicated habitual self-possession and self-respect. A high and intellectual forehead, a brow pensive but not gloomy, a mouth of inflexible decision, a face pale and worn but serene . . . Such was the aspect with which the great Proconsul presented himself to his judges."

No one then could possibly have foreseen the outcome of what was to prove the most bizarre political trial in British history. It was to last for the next seven years. When it was at last over, 60 of the peers present at the beginning—more than a third of them—were dead, and the Lord Chancellor had resigned. As for the unfortunate prisoner, he was old, worn out, and ruined.

It took two days to read the 20 Articles of Impeachment and the Answers. The first Article dealt with Benares; the second with the Begumis of Oudh; the sixth, part of the seventh and the fourteenth accused Hastings of taking bribes and presents; the fourth contained allegations relating to contracts alleged to have been improperly and improvidently given. Nothing was done to prosecute the others.

### A ravenous vulture

On February 15 Burke opened the general case. In emotion-charged oratory he described the history, constitution and conditions of eighteenth-century India. Although he had designed his speech on such a large scale that he had to curtail it, it still lasted for four full days.

For half a century after the trial of Hastings that opening speech was regarded as one of the classic orations of British history. The later verdict can only be that most of it was a masterpiece of overblown invective:

"He [Hastings] gorged his ravenous maw with an allowance of two hundred pounds a day. He is not satisfied without sucking the blood of fourteen hundred nobles. He is never corrupt without being cruel. He never dines without creating a famine.

"He feeds on the indigent, the decaying and the ruined, and then he depresses them together, not like the generous eagle who preys on a living, reluctant, equal prey; no, he is like the ravenous vulture, who feeds on the dead and enfeebled; who destroys and incapacitates nature in the destruction of its objects while devouring the carcasses of the dead, and then prides himself on his ignominious security. . . ."

Of the charges against Hastings, Burke continued: "They are crimes which have their rise in avarice, ferocity, malignity of temper, haughtiness, insolence; in short everything that manifests a heart blackened to the blackest, a heart dyed deep in blackness, a heart gangrened to the core . . .

"We have not chosen to bring before you a poor trembling delinquent . . . We have brought before you the head, the chief—one in whom all the fraud, all the tyranny of India are embodied, disciplined and arrayed."

Hastings had already submitted a paper in reply to the charges which, he said, were "not charges, but histories and comments".

"They are yet more; they are made up of mutilated quotations, of facts which have no mutual relation but are forced by false arrangement and connection, of principles of pernicious policy and false morality; assertions of guilt without proof or the attempt to prove them; interpretations of secret motives and designs which passed within my own breast, and which none but myself would know. . . ."

This reply, said Burke contemptuously, was merely "that indecent and unbecoming paper which lies upon our table". On February 18, the last day of his four-day oration, Burke ended venomously:

"**I charge** Mr. Hastings with having destroyed for private purposes the whole system of government by the six provincial councils which he had no right to destroy.

"**I charge** him with having delegated away from himself that power which the Act of Parliament had directed him to preserve inalienably within himself.

**PROSECUTION MANAGERS Charles Fox (left) and Burke (below) set about their task with relish. In the end they were revealed as oratorical hacks.**

Both Mary Evans

"I charge him with having formed a committee to be mere instruments and tools at the enormous expense of £62,000 a year.

"I charge him with having appointed a diwan [local ruler] to whom these Englishmen were to be subservient tools; whose name was abhorred and detested, stamped with infamy; and I charge him with giving him the whole power which he had thus separated from the Council General and from the provincial councils.

"I charge him with having taken bribes. I charge him with having done that service for the bribe iniquitously, and on behalf of the worst men.

"I charge him with having robbed those people of whom he took the bribes.

"I charge him with having fraudulently alienated the fortune of widows . . . with having, without right or title or purchase, taken the lands of orphans and given them to wicked persons under him.

"I charge him—his wickedness being known to himself and all the world—with

having committed to Deby Singh [a local ruler appointed by Hastings] the management of three great provinces and with having thereby wasted the country, destroyed the landed interest, cruelly harassed the peasants, burned their houses, seized their crops, tortured and degraded their persons, and destroyed the honour of the whole female race of that country. In the name of the Commons of England I charge with all this villainy on Warren Hastings."

### Theatrical performance

Then, after referring to the victims, prosecutors and judges, he ended: "I impeach him in the name of the Commons of Great Britain, whose Parliamentary trust he has betrayed, whose national character he has dishonoured.

"I impeach him in the name of the people of India, whose laws, rights and liberties he has subverted, whose properties he has destroyed, whose country he has laid waste and desolate.

**POPULAR PLAYWRIGHT Sheridan (above) and Prime Minister Pitt (left) are fortunate not to be generally remembered for their part in the Hastings affair.**

"I impeach him in the name of human nature itself, which he has cruelly outraged, injured and oppressed in both sexes, in every age, rank, situation and condition of life."

While this peroration was going on, ladies were in "a state of uncontrollable emotion" and "Mrs. Sheridan was carried out in a fit". There were frequent interruptions while the Lords applauded. As for Burke's physical condition:

"At the conclusion of the third morning it is true that his bodily powers becoming unequal to sustain so arduous an effort, he was compelled to postpone his further observations. But, resuming with new vigour the task on the following day, he finally accomplished it."

As soon as he sat down, a dispute began on procedure which quickly proved that while Burke could be a fashionable orator, he had no idea at all on how to manage a prosecution. As objection followed objection, and the managers were continually over-ruled, tempers became frayed.

Four months of this went by before Sheridan, the playwright, and a prosecution manager, rose to take the stage. "Accustomed to study theatrical effects at Drury Lane," an onlooker wrote, "he did not neglect to observe its principles or to practise its rules." Although 50 guineas were paid for seats at Sheridan's three-day speech, the Lords recognized it merely as a theatrical performance.

At the end of the first year of the trial only two of the 20 charges had been considered; at the end of the second year only two more had been passed. How long could this go on for, people began to ask; how much would it cost? Hastings, who had to foot his own bill, was already wringing his hands.

"My life will not be long enough, nor my fortunes sufficient to complete such a trial," he pleaded. "Had I pleaded guilty, my punishment could not have been greater."

The Lords shrugged their shoulders and went remorselessly on. At the end of the third year Parliament was dissolved. Could a new Parliament continue with an old impeachment, or would they have to begin all over again? It was a tricky question—occupying much of the following year's session. Fortunately it was decided that the impeachment could go on.

In the fourth year Hastings again pleaded for an end to his "torture". He told the Lords: "I am arraigned for desolating the provinces in India which are the most flourishing states in all of India. It was I who made them so. I gave you all, and you have rewarded me with confiscation, disgrace and a life of impeachment.

### Tedious evidence

"In no instance have I ever intentionally sacrificed the interests of my country to any private views of personal advantage . . . I have invariably promoted the happiness and prosperity of the people committed to my charge."

With regard to the tribute he had extracted from the rulers: "But for those sums of money I would not have been able to supply the armies in the field when they were in the last stage of exhaustion. My action was morally unassailable."

The trial dragged on for two more years of tedious evidence. On April 23, 1795 —in the sixth year of the proceedings— the 29 peers who were still interested enough to vote on a verdict acquitted Hastings of all the charges. It was ironic that his tormentor was not even present to see his triumph, for ten months earlier,

after a family bereavement, Burke had retired from the House of Commons and from politics.

After the verdict came the reckoning. The solicitor for the Commons assessed the prosecution's charges at £61,695, of which £16,996 was disallowed. For Hastings, with no taxpayers to back him, the defence had cost a staggering £71,080.

Facing complete ruin, the former Governor-General was eventually saved by his old employers, the East India Company. They gave him a pension of £4000 a year and paid the first ten years immediately.

Hastings retired from his ordeal into the country and made one brief and remarkable return to the political scene in 1813, when he was 81. The occasion was a Commons debate on the renewal of the East India Company's Charter, and Hastings was called to give evidence.

As he walked slowly to the Bar of the House, Members of Parliament on both sides rose to their feet in his honour. It was a single, short, and belated tribute to the central figure of the longest and most harrowing trial in criminal history.

**DIGNIFIED and determined, Hastings faced his malicious accusers and won— but the trial brought him financial ruin.**

National Portrait Gallery

# ANGELS FROM HELL

Despite the thick overlay of civilization which now covers most of the Western World, the primitive thirst for physical violence has not left us. In some cases it even appears to have become exacerbated by the pressures of modern life. Dirt, degradation and brutality are sometimes still applauded. . . .

UNTIL the Fourth of July riots in 1947 the only claim that Hollister, a small farming community of about 4000 people, ever had to fame was that it produced over 70 per cent of all the garlic consumed in America. As part of the Independence Day celebrations that year a motor-cycle hill climb was laid on for local enthusiasts. Word about it soon spread, however, and the town was flooded overnight with between three and four thousand motorcycle hoodlums who rampaged through the streets, brawling, boozing, molesting and "stomping" anyone who was foolish enough to get in their way.

The local police force, only seven men strong, could do nothing to stop them. Some stories say that the town was taken over completely. Even before it had blown over, the incident had gripped the imagination. Within a short time it was turned into celluloid history with the making of the Marlon Brando-Lee Marvin film *The Wild One*.

### Foreign battlefields

Not surprisingly, the contemporary Angels identify with Marvin's guttural violence and not with the "good" Brando. Although by today's standards it could never be classed as shocking, the film was banned for several years in Britain, and when it was finally released there was only one cinema in the country that would show it; needless to say, it played to capacity audiences.

It is probably no coincidence that the Hell's Angels of America have been spawned not once but several times in the past two decades. Each time it has been after the country's return or withdrawal from foreign battlefields. In the 'forties it coincided with the return of ex-G.I.s from the battlefields of the Second World War. Many wanted to settle down, but some had been completely uprooted and found peace-time living too undemanding; in the 'fifties the same pattern repeated itself with the ending of the Korean War and again in the 'sixties with Vietnam. Paradoxically, some Hell's Angels presidents demanded that they and their Chapters should be sent to Vietnam to show what they could do!

### Stink and dirt

The image that contemporary Angels have of themselves is of modern-day Texas Rangers, "James Brothers" and "Billy the Kids". They see themselves as continuing the old western tradition of violence and outlawry of which they claim to be part. Away from their large, heavy-duty motor cycles such as the Harley Davidson, they seem equally as strange as the cowboy without his horse. Whether the average law-abiding citizen will ever equate them with the glamorized thuggery of the present screen cowboys is doubtful. There are too many things against them.

To begin with, most people are turned off by the stink and dirt of their way of living. At initiation ceremonies initiates turn up in denim T-shirts, new Levis and sleeveless jackets. As part of the ritual acceptance, buckets of urine, vomit and excrement are tipped over their heads and on to their clothes, which are laid on the ground, and solemnly trodden in. These "originals", as the filth-covered garments are called, are worn until they rot. Until they do, they are regularly stiffened with crank-oil grease which they get from being laid under the bike to catch the drips. When they become too tattered to wear by themselves they are worn over a new pair of Levis.

Conventional leather gear and safety precautions such as motor-cycle helmets are never worn, although, from a practical point of view, it would be better to shed leather than skin: but nobody would be accepted into a Hell's Angels Chapter wearing such gear. The Angels claim to be the "One Percent" of American motor cyclists that are repeatedly condemned by officialdom. Their emblems or "colours" depict a winged skull wearing a motor-cycle helmet. The symbol is stitched to every garment, and an American cop who thought that he would make one guy take off every piece of clothing

**ANGELS IN ACTION . . . The film world tried (left and centre) to capture the "angel atmosphere", but the reality (left inset and below) is clearly different . . .**

Ronald Grant, Popperfoto, AP/Quartet

that showed the skull finally gave up when he found the "colours" tattooed across the jeering Angel's back.

Another favourite patch is the number 13 which is supposed to stand for the letter M, which is the thirteenth in the alphabet, and which in turn stands for marijuana, showing that the wearer uses the drug. Other favourite decorations are reproduction Nazi insignia such as swastikas and Iron Crosses. Popular ornaments are ear-rings and even occasional nose-rings, as well as long, heavy lengths of polished motor-cycle chain which are worn as belts but which can be unhooked in a moment and used as flails or bludgeons.

In a fight, whatever the rights or wrongs of an argument, the Angels stick by their motto of "All for One and One on All". They will, quite literally, stomp their opponents into the ground with fists, boots and chains.

### Drug scene

Each Chapter is controlled by a "President" and a "Serjeant-at-Arms" who is responsible for discipline. The name of individual Chapters, such as "Devil's Disciples" or "Satan's Sinners", is added under the colours. The blanket name of Hell's Angels is thought by the Angels themselves to have come from a California-based First World War bomber squadron who used to beat up aerodromes on their motor bikes in between flying sorties.

It is more probable that it was taken from a silent film of the period which was about a group of daredevil flyers called "Hell's Angels". Like so much else, its real origin will always be open to doubt.

Most Hell's Angels have criminal records of some sort. Generally they are for petty crimes such as stealing food, drink and petrol. In the past five years there is some evidence that they have begun to move in on the drug scene, although, as one policeman pointed out, using a Hell's Angel to smuggle drugs through customs is about as practical as sending through a lorry marked "Opium Express". The most frequent crime alleged against them is rape, and at the other end of the scale, cruelty to animals —a favourite practice being to bite the heads off living cockerels while posing for photographers with the blood trickling from the mouth.

Sometimes, when rape is alleged, the police investigation shows that a girl who has been willing to copulate with a trio of Hell's Angels has objected when she finds that she is expected to accommodate the whole Chapter. When the investigation does uncover a genuine case of rape, however, the details are pretty sickening. In one case, just five years ago, a teenage girl was repeatedly punched, kicked, whipped and raped in a "gang bang" lasting for 10 days. Even when she was hanging naked from the ceiling by her wrists she was forced to commit unnatural acts with some of the "old ladies" belonging to the Chapter.

The term "old ladies" is a contemptuous one, as is the other favourite expression for Angel women, which is

**MAD DOGS OF SUSSEX . . . They seem harmless enough (above), but one of their members, Brian Moore (inset left), slew Clive Olive (right) and is now in jail.**

"sheep". But there is a difference between the two. The "old ladies" are the recognized wives or mistresses. No one in the Chapter would think of interfering with another man's property while they were going steady. Yet the relationship in most cases is only temporary, lasting perhaps a week or a month. While it does, then the male exerts a fierce possessiveness. Some even demand that their girlfriends tattoo themselves on the inside of their thighs or directly above their pubis with phrases such as "Property of Maggot" to show ownership. Some girls have even included the motor-bike index number; one girl went so far as to re-register in this way every change of bike.

### Angel train

The other class of girl which hangs around the Hell's Angels Chapters is the "mamma" or "pussy", who is communal property and "there for the taking". These girls are the ones that are commonly involved in the "gang bang" or as it is more accurately known, "the angel train". They can be traded in for petrol, cash, spare motor-cycle parts or food. As they are often as unwashed, lice-ridden and diseased as the men, they do not get many men who are willing to trade for them outside their own circle.

Cases have been known where the men could not swap them for even half a gallon of petrol. The women's influence, it seems, is strictly limited to persuading the men to wash. In some Chapters the man who goes for a month without a wash gets a badge. As one horrified writer said, "God knows how much of a mess a man might appear if he set out for a row of medals."

But even the Angels' ability to shock is, it seems, limited. Very occasionally a particular piece of brutality highlights their activities, but claims that their nomadic existence represents a breakdown of society and the beginnings of reversion to a tribal existence are grossly exaggerated. One of the most noticeable things about the whole phenomenon of Hell's Angels is that they only flourish in large, open countries such as America or Australia where they can escape from towns and people.

What happens in closed communities such as Britain, where they don't have room to manoeuvre, is that their negative existence either takes on some of the standards of the society surrounding it or is confined to internecine warfare between rival Chapters. Essentially, they are no different from the earlier Teddy boys, Mods, Rockers and Skinheads. None of them can wield the crude strength of the American Hell's Angels in such a strait-jacketed society.

**Biggest clash**

Few British Angels possess a motor cycle—the prerequisite of any American Hell's Angel. Nor, it seems, can they shake off the conventional behaviour patterns. At a Rolling Stones concert in America the Hell's Angels acted as "bodyguards" and ended by stabbing someone to death during the performance. In Britain, when the Stones gave a similar concert in Hyde Park, the Hell's Angels co-operated with the police in making sure that people could get in and out freely and behaved in a relatively orderly manner.

Angel brutality in Britain has generally involved individual acts of violence. Hell's Angels became a popular press topic in December 1973 with the conviction of two former Hell's Angels for the murder of a 16-year-old boy whose trussed and weighted body was found in Shoreham Harbour, in southern England, in April that year.

The boy, Clive Olive, had drifted into the "Mad Dogs of Sussex" Chapter of Hell's Angels. According to his mother, some of them came from good homes, but they were content to drift along on social security or to live by petty thieving.

**ROCK FESTIVALS were a perfect target for Hell's Angels, but they often met with violent resistance from security guards in Britain, who proved too tough.**

Olive's murderer was Brian Moore, aged 21, a former Hell's Angel, who had been a keeper at Windsor Safari Park. After a row with a girl friend he tried to commit suicide by locking himself in a cage with two leopards and throwing the keys outside. His attempt failed for the simple reason that the leopards ignored him. He then began taking drugs, but was cured when he fell in love with a 16-year-old girl. He was furious when he heard that she had been raped, and it was this which led to the killing. After the murder, and after Moore had been sentenced, his father, according to a newspaper report, still thought that his son had been framed by Hell's Angels.

The biggest clash between British Chapters happened in Stevenage in July 1971, when two gangs, one known as "The Tongs" and the other as "The Scorpios", had a fight in a car park one Monday evening "because they were bored with new town life". Their weapons were a collection of belts, broken bottles, knives and bicycle chains. At the end of it the leader of "The Scorpios" lay dead with three stab wounds, one in the back. Three months later 28 of those who had taken part in the affray were gaoled. An 18-year-old boy is currently serving a life sentence for the murder. Yet none of them could be considered "genuine" Hell's Angels. They called themselves by the title but never went through the degrading initiation ceremonies. They liked the way that the Hell's Angels dressed, but that was as far as it went. Second-hand cars and mopeds were all the transport they had.

The tragedy of the whole incident was best summed up by a writer who said that "if the cult they chose to follow had not been one whose boastings of violence, sadism and aggression had been so spectacularly boosted by the media in the way that it was, it is worth considering whether that scuffle in the car park would have taken quite the form, and ended in quite the tragedy, that it did".

Unfortunately the one emotion that the Hell's Angels do not arouse is indifference.

Popperfoto

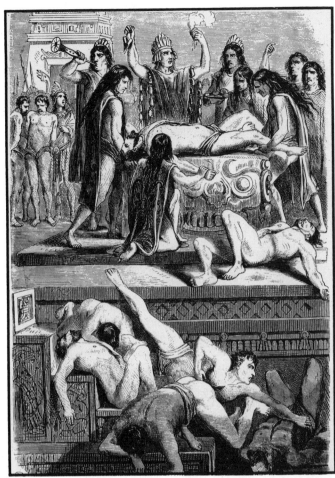

Mary Evans

# CANNIBALISM

Eating human flesh has always been considered a primitive custom. Yet there are plenty of examples of such behaviour in the so-called civilized world!

"I'VE got a problem," said the full-bearded young hippie. "I'm a cannibal." The policeman who had just arrested him looked at him incredulously. The man reached into his pocket and pulled out a number of small bones. "These aren't chicken bones. They're human fingers."

The conversation sounds like something out of a bad horror movie, but it took place on the afternoon of July 13, 1970, near Lucia, California, and the speaker was 23-year-old Stanley Dean Baker.

The case had started two days earlier, when a fisherman saw a human body caught in the reeds of the Yellowstone River, north of the Yellowstone National Park in Montana. When police waded into the river to recover the body, they realized this was no case of drowning. The corpse was clad only in underpants, and it had neither head nor arms. The legs had been severed at the knees. Where

**HUMAN SACRIFICE was a common religious procedure amongst the Incas and the Aztecs. Modern civilization has witnessed a number of similar practices.**

the heart should have been there was an ugly hole in the chest. Later in the day a coroner established that the man had been stabbed 25 times.

The absence of the heart suggested disturbing possibilities. Ever since the Manson case in 1969 California had been plagued with a rash of "ritual murders" — drug-ridden devil worship cults that offered human sacrifices in the manner of the ancient Incas and Aztecs. On Monday morning the police received a missing person report on Peter Schlosser, 22, who had driven off on Friday afternoon to camp in Yellowstone Park. He had been in a yellow sports car. This sounded as if it might be the victim. The

police put out an alarm call for a 1969 Opel Kadett car.

In fact the car was involved in an accident at about the time the alarm went out. Taking a corner on a dirt road too fast, it ran headlong into a pickup truck. The pickup was dented, but the sports car was almost a write-off. The driver of the pickup suggested they should drive to the nearest garage and send for a tow. The two hippies who had been in the sports car went with him; but while he was in the telephone booth, they disappeared, running towards the nearest woods.

Half an hour later it was established that the damaged sports car belonged to the murdered man. The hunt was on, and it ended quickly and anticlimactically when a patrolman saw two bearded hippies on a dirt road, ordered them to bend over his car with their hands on it, and radioed for help. It was as they

outs in the early 1960s; MacDonald also described getting up in the middle of the night and stabbing a sleeping man in a frenzy, and MacDonald attributed his fits of insane violence to a severe emotional shock in his teens—in this case, a homosexual rape.

But MacDonald—who was found to be insane—did not eat any part of his victims. His frenzy of destruction did not carry him that far. What is suggested by a comparison of the two cases is that cannibalism is a form of "ultimate destruction" of the victim. When head-hunting tribes in New Guinea eat their conquered enemies, the act symbolizes total conquest, total contempt; the enemy is not only defeated, he is digested and then excreted. It seems possible that the motive for the Yellowstone murder was Baker's hatred of the thoroughly "square" and respectable young man—Schlosser was an employee of the Mussel County Welfare Department at Roundup—the college graduate with his sports car, his horn-rimmed glasses, and his elaborate

**MODERN PRIMITIVES are still known to practise cannibalism in certain parts of the world. Above: A cannibal temple. Right: A skull rack—both in New Guinea.**

were driving into the Monterey police station that one of the men remarked: "I have a problem. I'm a cannibal," and confided that he had had a curious longing to eat human flesh ever since he received electric shock treatment for nervous disorder at the age of 17.

According to Stanley Dean Baker, his companion, Harry Stroup, had not been involved in the murder. He had been alone, he said, when Schlosser had offered him a lift on the previous Friday. All camping sites in the Yellowstone Park had been full, so they drove a few miles north and camped on the banks of the Yellowstone River. Schlosser had no suspicion that his companion was a homicidal maniac and a "devil worshipper".

In the middle of the night Baker shot his companion twice in the head with a .22 then stabbed him again and again with a hunting knife. He then cut up the body into six parts, severing the head, the arms and the legs. Baker alleged that he cut out the heart and ate it. Then, dropping a few severed fingers into his pocket, Baker threw the parts of the body into the river and drove off in the dead man's car.

In his possession when he was arrested was a paperback book, *The Satanic Bible,* a handbook of devil worship. Baker also stated that he had been on an "acid trip" shortly before the murder, having taken 65 doses of LSD. The murder brings to mind the case of the "Sydney mutilator", William MacDonald—the homosexual sadist who killed at least four down-and-

camping equipment. If this is true, it underlines one of the most disturbing trends in American crime in the 1970s, a trend that may be said to have started with the Manson "family" murders: the tendency of groups who feel themselves to be "social rejects" to lash out violently—and irrationally—at the "respectable" members of society.

The civilized response to cannibalism is always one of violent disgust; Alfred Packer and the *Mignonette* survivors aroused a public reaction of horrified fascination that was out of all proportion to the crimes committed. And this could well be because the thought of cannibalism stirs up deep, atavistic memories in human beings. There can be little doubt that our remote, cave-man ancestors were cannibals. In 1927 anthropologists discovered remains of Pekin Man, half a million years old, near Choukoutien, in China; they also discovered humanoid skulls that had been split open, and the brains extracted—suggesting that Pekin Man was a cannibal.

Similar evidence has revealed that Neanderthal Man and Cro-Magnon Man, *homo sapiens,* was also at times a cannibal. And in fact this is logical enough. Unlike the great apes, man has always been a flesh eater, and one of his earliest discoveries was how to wield a bone club to crack the skulls of his enemies. Since all food had to be hunted, what is more natural than that our ancestors should have eaten their enemies? Later on, when tribal customs and superstitions developed, men began to entertain a magical belief that to eat any living creature was one way of absorbing its qualities.

### Teeth marks

So, in many tribes, old people were eaten—rather than simply buried—because their children wanted to inherit their wisdom. The Greek historian Strabo declares that the tribes of Ireland practised cannibalism, while St. Jerome reports cannibalism in Scotland as late as the fourth century A.D. So we could say that it is only in fairly recent years that civilized man has given up the practice of eating his fellow men.

It is quite conceivable, therefore, that the explanation of Stanley Baker's cannibalism is not that black magic and LSD had driven him insane, but that they *released* some primitive, long-suppressed urge from his unconscious mind. The horror we feel when we read of cannibalism may be recognition that we are all capable of it.

This must be immediately qualified by stating that one form of cannibalism is purely sexual in origin. The Wisconsin necrophile, Ed Gein, arrested in 1957, was a sexually frustrated man who had for years been digging up newly buried

**NECROPHILE Ed Gein (above) got his kicks from sexual intercourse with dead bodies. He also murdered and stored the corpses in his lonely farmhouse (inset).**

female corpses, using them to satisfy his sexual needs and eating parts of them. The normal male sexual urge is, to some extent, a "sadistic" urge: that is to say, it is a desire to penetrate, to violate, the female. When a sexually aroused male presses the female violently against him, all his actions are basically aggressive.

In May 1971, 24-year-old Wayne Boden was arrested near Calgary, Canada, and charged with a series of rape murders. The first three victims were killed in Montreal; in each case there were teeth marks all over the breasts. The fourth victim, a schoolteacher, was found in Calgary, 2500 miles away, on May 18, 1971. The odd feature of the case was that in three of the four murders the victim had been "dating" her killer.

This was no case of a sex-starved psychopath grabbing a girl in a dark street, or bursting into her apartment; Boden was a good-looking, well-dressed, charming young man who would probably have had no difficulty in persuading most girls to satisfy normal sexual desires. But his desire was to use his teeth on the breasts and neck. Oddly enough, two of the four victims wore a faint smile, which suggests some degree of consent. Canadian newspapers dubbed Boden—sentenced to four terms of life imprisonment—the "Vampire rapist", but it would undoubtedly have been more accurate to call him the "Cannibal rapist".

And in the cases of Ed Gein and Albert Fish this "cannibal" element was taken to an extreme. It is an extension of the normal male desire to "wholly possess" a girl, and is a common feature of cases of sexual assault. Jack the Ripper claimed to have eaten a kidney taken from one of his victims. In *The Sexual Criminal*, Dr. Paul de River describes the case of a rapist who, after repeatedly violating his victim, also bit off her nipples and swallowed them. He also cites the case of a necrophiliac mortuary attendant who had for years been violating the corpses of young women.

This man frequently inserted a catheter into the bladder in order to drink the urine. He was finally caught because his sexual frenzy led him one day to bite the buttocks of a corpse so violently that the marks were observed by the embalmer. If, like Albert Fish, he had been able to continue to give outlet to his perverse desires, he might well have ended by committing murder and eating the body.

### Half dead

America's most famous "cannibal" was Alfred Packer, the prospector who killed and ate four of his companions. In the autumn of 1873 Packer was one of a party of 20 men who set out from Salt Lake City, Utah, hoping to find gold in the mountains of San Juan. As the winter drew on, they came close to starvation, and were saved only by a tribe of friendly Indians. Ten returned to civilization; another 10—with Packer as leader—pressed on. When Packer suggested that they should make for the source of the Rio Grande, four of the men declined to continue with him. These four later regretted their decision; caught in the winter snowstorms, two of them died, and the remaining two dragged themselves, half dead, into the Los Pinos Agency in February 1874.

In fact they had no reason to envy the others. All but Packer also met their deaths in the wilderness. A month after the two survivors had staggered into Los Pinos, another traveller came to the door, begging for food. It was Alfred Packer, and although he was obviously suffering from exhaustion, he looked fairly well fed. Packer's story was that the other five men had deserted him when he was ill. The men at the agency had no reason to doubt his story. Ten days later, Packer went on to Saquache, and began to drink heavily.

### Headless corpse

He seemed to have plenty of money. The stories he told of his ordeal varied so much that people began to suspect foul play. He was arrested by General Adams, from the Agency, and held on suspicion. On April 2 two excited Indians rushed into the Agency holding strips of flesh which they said they had found outside. They said it was "human meat". Packer fainted. When he recovered, he told a strange story of cannibalism. They had been starving in the mountains and were living on roots. One day, when he had been out gathering firewood, he returned to the camp to find that the oldest man in the party, Israel Swan, had been murdered with a blow on the head, and the others were engaged in cutting up the body to eat it.

Swan's money—$2000—was divided equally. Packer ate part of Swan. When this food ran out, a man called Miller was killed with a sudden blow with a

**RESCUE! Survivors of the Uruguayan plane crash are brought down from the Andes (above). They were saved by the efforts of Parrado and Canessa (left).**

Both AP

hatchet—he was the fattest. After Miller was eaten it was the turn of a man called Humphrey; then Noon. This only left Packer and a companion named Bell; they agreed not to try to kill one another. But one day, said Packer, Bell had attacked him in a frenzy, and he had been forced to kill him with a hatchet. He cut strips of flesh from the body, and continued his journey until he saw the Agency ahead—and then threw away the flesh.

The next day Packer led a party back into the mountains; but he claimed he was unable to remember the scene of the murder. That night he tried to kill the man to whom he was handcuffed and escape, but he was detected in time.

The five corpses were found in June, near the shores of Lake Christoval. It was immediately clear that Packer had lied. Four of the five had been shot in the back of the head. Miller's corpse was headless, but when the head was found, it was seen that he had been killed with a violent blow from the butt of a rifle. The ribs of all the dead men were exposed; evidently Packer's preference had been for the flesh of the breast. Blankets were found in a nearby cabin; Packer had lived there after the murders, making trips back to the frozen bodies for meat.

Packer's second attempt to escape was successful, and he was not caught again until January 29, 1883, nine years later. He had been recognized at Cheyenne, Wyoming; he was suspected of being a member of a gang of outlaws. He was tried for the murder of only one of the men, Israel Swan, and sentenced to death. However, at a retrial he was charged only with manslaughter, and sentenced to 40 years in jail. He received a pardon 18 years later, and died near Denver in 1907.

Packer undoubtedly murdered his five companions, and the crime *is* horrifying. Yet the charge of manslaughter suggests that the prosecution found it impossible to believe that anyone would eat human flesh for pleasure. Packer undoubtedly decided that they would all die of cold and starvation, and that if he hastened their deaths he alone might survive. This has been the motive in most of the cases of cannibalism by civilized human beings.

Certainly the most moving and remarkable of these was one that took place in the winter of 1972, when a planeload of survivors lived for 10 weeks in the Andes on the flesh of their companions. The Uruguayan plane, en route to Chile, crashed in the Andes with 45 people on board. After 10 days, the survivors reluctantly decided that their only chance of survival was to eat their dead companions. When they heard on the plane radio that the rescue search had been called off, there seemed no alternative to starving to death or eating their companions in order to live.

### Exposure

Three of the men climbed higher up the mountain, and concluded that the wreck of their plane could not be seen from the air. One by one the badly injured died, until there were 27 of the original 45 left. A landslide of snow half-buried the plane and suffocated eight more of the party, including Liliana Methol, the last woman survivor—her husband, Javier Methol, was one of the few to get back to civilization. One of the 19 survivors recalled the words of a taxi-driver, that the snow stops and the summer starts in the Andes on November 15; this was October 31, and the thought gave them hope.

Occasionally they cooked the human flesh; but they had too little fuel to indulge in this luxury frequently. It was near the end of the first week of December that birds circled above their camp, and they realized that spring was at last approaching. Three more deaths from exposure decided three of the men to make an attempt to reach civilization and bring rescuers. Roberto Canessa, Nando Parrado and Antonio Vizintin set off to climb the mountain—the first steps of a westward route—using cushions as snowshoes. It took them most of three days to reach the summit; and when Parrado reached it he saw nothing but snow-capped mountains ahead.

### Sausage-meat

However, far to the west there were two mountain peaks that were not covered with snow. They had only enough food for 10 days, and the mountains looked as if they were at least two months' march away. They decided that Vizintin should return to the plane. Then the other two plodded on. For another week they continued, down the mountain and along a river valley, and finally the sight of a rusty horseshoe and a soup can told them they were close to civilization.

On December 20, 10 days after setting out, they saw three men on horseback on the other side of the river—peasants. The next day a poor peasant rode up to them, gave them cheese—and went on up the valley to inspect his cows. Later, they returned with him to his wooden hut—and finally, after 10 weeks, ate a normal meal. It was December 21. A Chilean airforce helicopter rescued the

**ALMOST unbelieving relief on the face of the Andes survivor. His rescue from the prospect of further cannibalism and final starvation must have seemed a miracle.**

remaining 13 survivors on the following day. Of the original 45, only 16 returned to civilization. They had survived largely on the bodies of the other 29.

From the strictly criminal point of view there have been few notable cases involving cannibalism. Fish, Gein and Stanley Baker were all undoubtedly insane, and it could therefore be argued that they should be regarded as madmen rather than criminals. But four other cases should be noted briefly. In 1897 Adolph Leutgart, a sausage manufacturer of Chicago, murdered his second wife, Louise, and dumped her body in a vat he used for boiling sausage-meat.

Many Chicagoans still refer to Leutgart as the man who turned his wife into sausages. In fact, this is untrue; he poured caustic potash on the body and boiled it. After a few days all that remained of his wife were two gold rings in the bottom of the vat. However, this was enough to convict Leutgart, who died in prison before he could be executed. He explained the murder by saying he was "possessed by the devil".

### Pickled bodies

Fritz Haarmann, the Hanover butcher who killed youths and sold their bodies for meat, had two remarkable German contemporaries, Karl Denke, of Münsterberg, and George Grossmann, of Berlin. Both killers were caught—Grossmann in August 1921 and Denke in December 1924—when sounds of a struggle led other tenants to investigate their rooms. Denke was in the process of killing a young journeyman; Grossmann had already killed a girl.

Denke's house was found to contain two large tubs of brine, in which various parts of male bodies were pickled. Denke had kept a detailed record of 30 victims, mostly down-and-outs, whom he had killed and partly eaten. Grossmann, who specialized in picking up young girls—preferably fat—at the railway station, had killed a dozen women and sold their bodies for meat, as well as eating parts himself. Both hanged themselves in prison before they could be executed.

### Daylight

We may regard cannibalism as a terrible, dark survival of man's animal past, lurking like some sinister monster in the depths of the subconscious. But a healthier view is put by the anthropologist A. I. Hopkins, who points out that directly a primitive tribe comes into contact with civilization, cannibalism disappears of its own accord. "Directly daylight falls on the habit, it withers away." Study of the history of cannibalism suggests that these sane, balanced words come closer to the basic truth about human nature.

# HUNGER FOR HUMAN FLESH

The hard-bitten pioneers who opened up the West often endured terrible hardships on their long trek to California. None, however, suffered like the infamous Donner wagon-train, or stooped so low in order to survive . . .

Bettmann Archive

WINTER had come early to the high peaks of the Sierra Nevada, the last great barrier on the 1846 emigrant trail that stretched the 2000 miles from Missouri to California. By late October, snow had already closed most of the passes through the 10,000-ft. mountain range. Until the snows melted in the following spring, there would be no way through for the sturdy pioneers streaming westwards to California's "promised land". The wagon train season was over.

Over, that is, except for one party which even then was struggling upwards along Nevada's Truckee River, on the wrong side of the mountains. Of the 87-strong company that had set out for the West with their sturdy ox-teams and high-wheeled wagons that summer, five had already died on the gruelling journey. Out in the Nevada and Utah deserts their graves and abandoned personal belongings bore mute testimony to the hardships the emigrants had undergone.

As their leader, 62-year-old former Illinois farmer George Donner, urged his charges along, he could see the snow plumes whipped up by the fierce winds in the Sierra peaks ahead. He was filled with foreboding.

**Desperate situation**

Sitting beside him in the lead wagon, his wife Tamsen glanced back at the handful of wagons remaining from the 20 that had set out. Then the company had been cheerfully looking forward to their new life in California. Now, after the slow, tortuous desert crossing—first lost, then back on the trail, then lost again—they were seriously behind schedule. Worse still, Indians had taken toll of their precious stock, and they were now very short of food.

Further back in the line, blond-haired Lewis Keseberg was easing his wagon over the difficult and rocky scrub. At the age of 32 this German from Westphalia was on his way to California with his wife, Phillipine, and their two small children. Keseberg and Mr. and Mrs. Donner were to play an important part in the drama that was about to unfold.

On October 30 the party reached Truckee Lake, 6000 ft. up in the mountains, with the snow already beginning to fall around them. George and Tamsen Donner had by then fallen back in the line, ready to assist the weaker wagon teams which were trailing along exhausted, up to five miles behind the main party. It was clear to all that the situation was becoming desperate, and their progress became slower and slower. As they camped amid the snowstorm that night they realized that they would have to go on the next day, whatever the weather.

When they woke in the morning, the storm which had come upon them during the night had done its damage. Around the camp, where they had huddled together for protection, the snow had drifted to a depth of 10 feet. There was no way in which their cumbersome wagons could go forward. Gathering their precious possessions together, those at the front of the party decided to attempt the summit pass that lay between them and safety, on foot.

As they plunged through the chest-high drifts, their clothing soaked by the treacherous, feathery snow, the terrible truth became apparent—they were trapped. Four desperate days later, on November 3, 1846, they finally gave up and made their dejected way back to the wagons they had abandoned by Truckee Lake. Here, and in another camp some miles back on the trail, they camped. Eighty-two men, women, and children—there were many children—lay trapped in a winter fastness, with insufficient food, yet only a day's normal journey from safety across the pass.

There was to be nothing normal, however, about that winter in the Sierra Nevada. Before it was over, the fate of many of the Donner party was to be sealed, and a human drama would unfold that included not just heroism, but robbery, murder, and cannibalism—the last on a scale not seen before or since in modern society.

At first, life in the camps was comparatively normal. The Kesebergs, and other families such as the Breens, Reeds, and Murphys, built and occupied three rude log cabins, close to the lakeside. Together they formed a community of 60, of which 29, nearly half, were children. Five miles downstream, George and Tamsen Donner had built their own settlement, which housed the 21 people—including 12 children—who had travelled in their personal group.

## Intense hunger

With the smoke rising from the fires of each community, and with pet dogs still to be found round the cabins and lean-tos, a casual observer would have been forgiven for assuming that all was well. Reality was very different, however. What meagre supplies they had brought with them were by now exhausted. Only their pack animals, oxen, and family pets stood between them and the threat of starvation.

By November 12, weakened by the cold and the storm that had raged intermittently until the previous day, it was clear that—unless some could escape and bring help—they were destined to die. Accordingly, 13 of the strongest men and two of the strongest women set off through the snows for the pass, carrying what little dried ox meat could be spared. Both this, and a similar attempt a week

PERILS of all kinds faced the intrepid emigrants of the Old West, and thousands died on the way not just as a result of Indian hostilities but also through lack of supplies of water or simply inadequate planning for the trip.

later, failed completely.

Finally, on December 14, after more than six weeks of blizzard and starvation, the emigrants at the camp by the lake made their decision. Using roughly fashioned snowshoes, those adults with sufficient strength left would make a "do-or-die" dash across the mountains to safety. On the clear but freezing morning of December 16, 10 men, two youths, and five of the younger women set out. Behind them, at the lake, they left Lewis Keseberg in charge of the men too weak to move, the remaining women, and the children. From the Donner camp, five miles downtrail, there had been no word for weeks.

At first they made good progress, though two men decided to turn back at the end of the second day. Then, remorselessly, the effects of their ordeal began to be felt as they stumbled and slithered their way through the dazzling white snowfield of the summit. Intense hunger pains gnawed at their stomachs, they began to hallucinate, to slide down the slippery slope of starvation towards death.

## Brother's heart

Christmas Day, 1846, saw them crouched under the inadequate shelter of a thin blanket, while yet another mountain storm raged round them. Three men were already dead. Of the others, those who were not delirious began to eye one another nervously. The same single thought ran through their heads.

William Eddy, a once sturdy farmer from Illinois, was the first to voice it. With his sunken eyes firmly fixed on the pathetic fire in front of him, he spoke. "There is nothing left to eat," he said, "but ourselves." For a moment there was silence. Beside him, Patrick Dolan was already deep in a starvation coma. If they did not rouse him there would soon be food of a kind for all.

The day after Christmas, as the storm died down, they took the final step. Weeping with emotion, they cut the flesh from the arms and legs of the now-dead Dolan's body and roasted it over the fire. Civilized man's strongest taboo had been irrevocably broken. The next to die was 12-year-old Lemuel Murphy. That same evening, as she crouched by the fire, his married sister Sarah looked with horror at the object that spat and sizzled in the embers. It was her kid brother's heart.

For three days they rested among the stunted pines of the primitive mountain camp. Of the 15 who had been on the mountain, five were already dead—one lost in the snows, and four cut, broiled and packed for the hard journey that still lay ahead. The five men remaining, William Eddy, Sarah's 28-year-old husband William Foster, Jay Fosdick, and two Indian guides, knew that this would not be enough.

Indeed, by the evening of January 1, 1847, the 10 survivors had eaten the last of the cooked and dried human flesh that had been their only food for a week. As he forced the final, half-masticated piece down his throat, William Eddy looked across at Jay Fosdick. It was obvious that he could not last long. But after him, what then? The rest of the party all seemed discouragingly "healthy".

Suddenly, William Foster spoke out. "If any of us are going to survive, one of us will have to be killed." His matted hair and staring blood-shot eyes gave him the appearance of a madman. "We should draw lots for it. No, wait a moment. I have a better idea. Let us kill the Indians." Away from the main group, the two Indians who had volunteered to guide them through the mountains sat on their own. Foster meaningfully patted the pistol in his belt.

Thus the last veneer of civilization was finally stripped away. The half-crazed and starving emigrants had moved from eating human flesh, through a week of watching and hoping that another of their number might die, to murder—not murder for revenge or gain, but for the bodies of the victims themselves.

Even then they rationalized it out. To kill an Indian would not be like killing a white man. Had not the Indians on the overland trail stolen their cattle? It could hardly be called murder. Eddy was appalled. These men had stood by them through all but unendurable hardships.

That night he warned the two Indians that their continued presence would put their lives in danger. Under cover of darkness they crept from the camp. As the dawn came up over the desolate snowscape, only the bloodstained tracks of their rock-torn and frost-bitten feet remained to show their direction.

## Double murder

For a short while the problem was eased by the death of Jay Fosdick. With three less mouths to feed there was at least some human flesh for the seven survivors. They knew, however, that Fosdick's emaciated corpse would not last them long. By now they had become experts in the "housekeeping" of cannibalism.

On January 9 fate finally caught up with the faithful Indian guides. As the party staggered along through the snows that led to safety, they came across the fresh tracks of the two men. Tearing the pistol from his belt, Foster, by now quite mad, half ran and half lurched forward. There, under the trees, were the two Indians, completely exhausted.

As Foster came upon them, the first Indian weakly propped himself up on one elbow. Looking up, he found the gun levelled at his forehead. That was the last thing he ever saw. A split-second later he was dead. The second Indian was given only slightly longer to make his peace. Then, as he gazed exhaustedly at the body of his fellow tribesman, Foster shot him through the head.

Just before the two shots rang out, the rest of the party had turned their backs. At least they could later claim that they were not eye-witnesses, should they ever escape from the wilderness. This calculated act of double murder split the party into two groups: Eddy and three of the women, who thereafter camped some distance from Foster, and Foster and the two women who travelled with him. For the Fosters, at least, there was now sufficient meat to see them through. For Eddy and his companions there were the dried remains of Fosdick.

## Filth and squalor

Ten days later the survivors staggered into Johnson's Ranch—the first settlement in the Sacramento Valley—starved, smeared with blood, and half-naked. For their 33 days in the snows the two men and five women had existed on a staple diet of human flesh. When that had run out, they had killed to obtain more. Horrifying though it was, the tragic story of the Donner party was just unfolding.

Across the mountains, in the snowbound camps by the lake, the main group waited for news that the escape bid had been successful. Through December and January, they had been reduced to eating the hides that formed the roofs of their primitive shelters. As the gaunt figures shuffled through the snow, among the filth and squalor surrounding the camps, it seemed that rescue would never come. Unknown to them, however, relief was on the way.

Alerted by Eddy's escape, a rescue party was steadily pushing its way through the Sierras from the Californian side. Loaded down with precious supplies, they finally crossed the pass to Truckee Lake on February 18, 1847. The scene at the camps was appalling. Many had died of starvation. Their bodies lay stretched out on the snow, as the others had not had the strength to bury them.

It was clear that all those who could, should attempt to get out—however hard the conditions. Twenty-four emaciated, hardly recognizable humans assembled to make the journey. Behind them they left the dead, and the final 32 men, women, and children who would have to wait for further rescue attempts. There was not sufficient food to give any to those remaining by the lake.

Although 22 of the 24 travellers survived the crossing, what happened to those still in the camps sets the seal on

VICTIM of a series of unforeseen difficulties, the Donner party (below) was way behind schedule when it finally arrived at the towering Sierra Nevada . . .

EMACIATED, exhausted and well-aware of how his fellows managed to survive, William Eddy (left) found help and later emerged as the episode's only male hero.

Bettmann Archive

Culver

the horror that later became known as the Donner Party. On March 1 a second, stronger party made yet another trip along the body-strewn escape trail. As they looked down on the camps that morning, an ominous stillness filled the air.

Coming closer, they could discern feeble movements among the cabins. In one lay the body of Milt Elliott, a teamster who had elected to stay behind. Although the head and face were untouched, most of the flesh had been torn from the rest of the body. Bones and half-chewed muscle lay strewn about the cabin floor. Elsewhere there were tufts of different-coloured hair. Cannibalism had come to the camps.

Some distance away, at the camp containing the Donners and their relatives, the story was the same. As the rescuers approached, their first sight was of a figure calmly walking across the snow, carrying the leg of a man cut off at the thigh. In a hastily dug hole was the rest of George Donner's older brother Jacob—in pieces. He had succumbed to cold and starvation, and it was his meat that stocked the Donner "larder".

### Savage air

Once more the rescuers acted with all speed. By March 3 most of the survivors were on their way over the pass. Then, a storm broke, fiercer and heavier than any that had burst over the Sierras that winter. As they huddled round their camp fire they knew that for many this was the end. Gradually the fire burnt deeper and deeper into the snow, and the weaker members of the party sank into a stupor. By morning, with their food gone, what had originally been a well-planned rescue attempt had lapsed into chaos.

Two of the 14 who had started out were dead. Crouched in the fire pit, now some 25 feet deep, young Mary Donner made the first suggestion. From the lips of this innocent, seven-year-old child came the words: "We'll have to eat the dead people." Under an hour later the corpse of 47-year-old Elizabeth Graves lay dismembered, as her breasts, liver, and heart cooked slowly over the fire. Her one-year-old baby sat beside her mother's body.

When the survivors were eventually rescued, Mrs. Graves and two children had died, and their bodies had been eaten. The remaining 11 were too shocked and exhausted to talk of their experience. Once the taboo had been broken, it seemed that there was to be no end to the cannibalism.

In a more ominous way, events were repeating themselves back at the camps. Here Lewis Keseberg had been left, together with the Donners and others, to await a third rescue bid. Tamsen Donner had stood up to the rigours of the winter well, despite her ghastly and unnatural diet of human flesh. Loyally, she had refused the chance of escaping, to tend her husband who was gradually dying from a gangrenous arm. This loyalty was to cost her her life.

Keseberg was not recognizable as the arrogant young German who had started the journey. His matted hair and beard gave him a savage air, which was beginning to be matched by his behaviour. One night he had taken young George Foster, a toddler aged four, to bed with him. The next morning the lad was dead. Though nothing could be proved, the suspicion was that he had been murdered. Keseberg, at any rate, was unmoved. In full view of the others, he hung the child's body upside down on the cabin wall, and prepared to eat him.

### Two cauldrons

On March 13 the final rescue party broke through to bring out the remaining people. More had died, more had been eaten. This was definitely the last chance there would be of rescue until the spring melted the Sierra snows. Tamsen Donner yet again refused to leave her dying husband. Three times now she had demonstrated her iron-willed loyalty.

Eventually, a compromise was reached. Tamsen Donner stayed behind to nurse George; Lewis Keseberg remained sulking in the cabin of the elderly, dying Mrs. Murphy; two of the strongest rescuers were deputed to look after them all. If they could hang on for another month, the mountains would be clear of snow. However, as the last line of people disappeared from view, so did the two men who had been detailed to organize the camp. With no thought for their charges, they had gathered up what loot they could carry from the emigrants' possessions and made for the pass and safety. Plucky Tamsen Donner's fate was sealed.

As to what happened next, there were no witnesses. On March 19 the ailing Mrs. Murphy died. From then on, three characters took the stage for the last act of the drama. At the camp by Lake Truckee, Lewis Keseberg was sustaining himself on the remains of Mrs. Murphy. Almost five miles away, Tamsen Donner was coming to the end of her weary vigil at the deathbed of her husband.

Some time in the afternoon of March 26, it would appear, Mrs. Donner arrived at Keseberg's cabin. Her husband George had died. Now she and Keseberg were the only two people left alive the other side of the mountains.

When, on April 17, 1847, yet another party reached the lake from California, they found only one person alive—Lewis Keseberg. Since, only a month before, Tamsen Donner had been by far the healthiest survivor in the camps, their suspicions were aroused. In Keseberg's cabin they discovered other evidence that pointed to a possible, macabre end to Mrs. Donner's life.

There, among the rotting debris to which both rescuers and survivors had by now become accustomed, were two small cauldrons full of human blood, together with a simmering pan of fresh liver and lights. Of Tamsen Donner there was no trace. Questioning Keseberg closely, they established that Mrs. Donner was indeed dead. She had, according to Keseberg, wandered off into the snow and died of exposure.

"So what," they questioned, "has happened to Mrs. Donner's body?" Keseberg waved his hand towards the pan with its gruesome contents. In his guttural German accent he said: "Some of her is in there. The rest I have eaten. She was the best I have ever tasted." Threats, even the threat of death, could not make Keseberg expand on his story. Even the subsequent discovery that he had much of Mrs. Donner's property in his possession could wring nothing more from him than his original statement.

April 25 found the three rescuers and the one remaining survivor ready to leave the camp from which 42 had already died. The melting snows revealed the remains of dismembered corpses, the mute testimony to the suffering, cannibalism, and murder that had occurred there. Just before they left, they put one final question to Keseberg. Why was it, when the thaw had revealed frozen horse and ox meat, that he had persisted in his diet of human flesh?

### Pitiful epitaph

His answer was spine-chilling. "I tried them," he said, "and they were too dry for my taste. Human liver and lights are far more tasty. And as for human brains (the lovingly laid-out body of George Donner had been found with its skull split open and the brains removed), well, they make the best soup of all."

In any ordinary society there is little doubt that Keseberg would have stood trial for the murder of Tamsen Donner. But the California of the 1840's was no ordinary society. The rule of law had not yet arrived with the wagon trains. Instead, Keseberg went free. To those who claimed he was a murderer he had one answer. He sued them; only to be awarded a derisory one dollar damages.

For Tamsen Donner there was a pitiful epitaph. As Keseberg, in later years, went the rounds of California's bars, he would boast: "That was the healthiest woman I ever ate. I boiled out four pounds of fat from her body." Early in the 1850's he achieved one of his life's ambitions—he opened a steakhouse, serving the "finest and tenderest" of meat.

THE FATEFUL ROUTE, followed by Donner party (above are sections from a map of their route), which was to end in disaster. Left is a sketch of Keseberg, who said he actually preferred the taste of human flesh. He symbolized the degredation of the doomed group. Ironically, he set up a steakhouse when he finally reached California.

Culver Pictures

# A MILD-MANNERED MONSTER

When police finally caught up with the killer of 10-year-old Grace Budd they stared at him in blank amazement. He was a smartly dressed, kindly old man with a gentle, if rather absent, smile. Perhaps there had been a mistake . . . By the time of the trial, however, a good deal of fresh evidence had accumulated. And it suggested not only that the old man was guilty, but that he was one of the most horrifying sexual monsters in criminal history — and a cannibal as well!

LITTLE is known of the background of young Grace Budd, except that she lived with her parents and older brother in a shabby apartment in down-town New York, where the sun seldom penetrated the dirt-encrusted windows, and where her family eked out a typically precarious existence in the poverty-stricken America of the late 1920s.

Little, that is, apart from the events of Sunday, June 3, 1928 — the last day of her life, and one which was to result in one of the country's strangest murder trials more than six years later.

On that day a small, elderly, grey-haired man, calling himself "Frank Howard", had visited the Budd household in response to a newspaper advertisement placed by 18-year-old Edward Budd looking for work. He was, explained "Mr. Howard", a vegetable farmer, and could offer young Budd a job in the country. So persuasive and charming was the elderly stranger that the Budds allowed him to take their 10-year-old daughter, Grace, to a children's party that very afternoon. She was never seen alive again.

Nearly seven years later, in a stifling courtroom in Westchester County, New York State, the savage story of the end of Grace Budd was slowly and remorselessly revealed.

As the District Attorney rose to deliver his opening address the atmosphere was tense. The 20 reporters crowded round the small baize table at the front of the court leant forward expectantly, their ties loosened, their pencils poised over their notebooks.

The tall, burly man cleared his throat: "May it please the court, Mr. Foreman, and gentlemen of the jury. The defendant, Albert Howard Fish, is charged with murder in the first degree, in that he choked to death one Grace Budd, in the town of Greenburgh, in this county."

Across from him, at the defence table, sat the accused, a small, elderly man, so meek that one would not think evil of him. Yet 65-year-old, Albert Fish — a grandfather five times over — was to be revealed by his own confession as a criminal pervert, cannibal, and monster. The District Attorney continued:

"The People will prove that the defendant, on his own admission, appeared at the apartment of Albert Budd, the

victim's father, on the afternoon of June 3, 1928, and took his daughter Grace, then a child not yet 11 years old, away with him to Greenburgh, to an unoccupied house known as Wisteria Cottage, where he choked the life from her."

Fish sat impassively, absent-mindedly fingering his trim moustache, as if he had not heard one word of the dreadful indictment that had been laid against him.

"Nothing has been seen of Grace Budd from that day to this," the District Attorney continued. "When the defendant took her away that afternoon, ostensibly to a party at his sister's, her fate was sealed. Despite urgent police enquiries, no trace could be found of her for over six years, until a letter arrived at the Budds' home on November 11, 1934, addressed to Mrs. Budd."

### "She died a virgin"

He leant forward and drew an envelope from the briefcase on the desk in front of him. "With the court's permission, I will read this letter to the jury. It is, gentlemen, unsigned, but you will later hear evidence that it, and the envelope it came in, has been traced to the defendant.

"'Dear Mrs. Budd. Some years ago a friend of mine, Captain John Davis, shipped from California to Hong Kong, China, where at that time there was a great famine. It was dangerous for children under 12 to be on the streets, as the custom was for them to be seized, cut up, and their meat sold for food. On his return to New York, my friend seized two boys, one six and the other 11, killed, cooked, and ate them.

"'So it was that I came to your house on June 3, 1928, and under the pretence of taking your daughter Grace to a party at my sister's I took her up to Westchester County, to an empty house up there, and I choked her to death. I cut her up and ate part of her flesh. I did not have sex with her. She died a virgin.'"

### Five minutes

Dramatically, he slammed the letter down on the table and shot a scathing glance at the hunched figure of Fish across the room, who still seemed unmoved by the events. "Call Detective Smith to the stand." The District Attorney's voice pierced the silence of the courtroom. A tall, portly figure took the witness chair. "You are a detective attached to the New York City police force?" "Yes, sir." "Then tell us of the events of December 13 last, and what led up to them."

Hands clasped, the detective spoke in a soft, firm voice: "When Mrs. Budd received the letter, she contacted me at once. I had been originally assigned to the case, and the file remained open. From an imperfectly erased address on the back of the envelope I managed to trace the

defendant to an apartment on 52nd Street. On the morning of December 13 I arrested him and took him down to headquarters, where he voluntarily made a statement."

"What was in that statement?" The lawyer's face was tense.

"Well, sir, he said he had left a bundle, containing a butcher's knife, a cleaver, and a saw, by a news-stand on the corner of the Budds' apartment block. After he had taken the Budd child away, he travelled with her on the 'El' (New York's old elevated railway), and then on the New York Central, to Greenburgh. They left the train together and went to a house there, known as Wisteria Cottage. He said that he took her into a room there, and that he choked her to death. The choking took about five minutes."

The officer paused, looking round nervously at the women in the public gallery. He continued: "Then, sir, he took off her clothes and cut her head off with the cleaver. Then he sawed her in two, across the body above the navel, and left the lower part of the body behind the door in the room. The head he wrapped in paper, and hid behind the cistern in the outside lavatory." Suddenly the atmosphere in the courtroom had taken on an icy chill.

"Three or four days later, he cannot remember which, he returned to the house and threw all three sections of the body over the stone wall that runs behind it. After making the statement, he was taken to the spot where he said the body lay, and we found the bones of a young female, aged about 10, cut just as he had described."

### Prolific killer

The District Attorney held out a large, labelled cardboard box. Taking off the lid, he turned to the detective. "Would these be the bones, officer?" "Yes, sir, I recognize the official label." As the lawyer returned the box to the table the jury distinctly heard the rattling of the remains in the stillness of the courtroom. "Did the defendant afterwards add anything to that statement?"

"Yes, sir, in all he made six formal confessions to the murder while in our custody, adding details as the confessions went along. He also said that he was sorry he had killed her, and that he would have done anything to bring her back to life."

The case against Fish was stark in its completeness. The man had confessed, first in the letter to Mrs. Budd and then six times to the police. His confession had been corroborated by the remains found at the scene of the crime, and by tracing the letter and envelope back to him. Against such a weight of evidence there could be only one defence: a plea of insanity. To support its contention

that Fish was insane, the defence called as a witness Dr. Frederic Wertham, one of the foremost psychiatrists in America.

When he took the stand, Dr. Wertham knew more about Fish's mental state than anyone else in court, on either side. On first meeting him in his prison cell, soon after his arrest, Fish had struck Dr. Wertham, as he later recalled, as "a meek and innocuous little old man. Gentle and benevolent, friendly and polite. If you wanted someone to entrust your children to, he would be the one you would choose."

What Dr. Wertham learnt from many sessions with the prisoner was to transform one sordid crime into the very real possibility that he was dealing with the most prolific child killer in American criminal history.

### Naked

First he gave his version of Fish's story, as told to him in the grim confines of his cell. It was cold, simple and, in Dr. Wertham's opinion, bore the mark of madness.

"He has told me," he said, "that he feels driven to torment and kill children. Sometimes he would gag them, tie them up and beat them, though he preferred not to gag them, as he liked to hear their cries. In this case his original intentions were to take Grace's brother and castrate him — he claims he is ordered by God to castrate small boys — but Edward Budd was too large.

"Instead he took Grace. He explains that he had to sacrifice her to prevent her future outrage in the adult world. He felt that this was the only way in which she could be saved. That is why he killed her.

"On the day of the murder, when they arrived at the house, he took his implements inside and stripped. The child was out in the sunshine picking flowers. He went to the window and called out to her; when she came in and saw him naked she screamed that she would tell her mother.

### Complete insanity

He grabbed her by the throat, threw her to the floor, and strangled her. It was, he says, 'to put her out of her misery'." By now the jury were concentrating intently on Dr. Wertham's words. The police confessions were routine, but here was the testimony of an expert who had delved deep into Fish's twisted mind.

"He took parts of her body home with him, and cooked them in various ways. Then, over a period of nine days, he ate the flesh by day, and thought about it by night, during all which time he was in a

**SUSPICION was far from the minds of the Budd family (right) when Fish called on them. But young Grace (ringed) ended up as a gruesome meal in a stewpot . . .**

UPI

state of intense sexual excitement.'' With Dr. Wertham's words a shudder ran through the court.

He had more, much more, to add on the strange life of Albert Fish—information so revolting that often the court was cleared during the many hours in which he was on the witness stand. Sentence by sentence the picture was built up of complete insanity.

## An active pervert

Albert Fish had done many things in his life. At the age of 15 he worked in a grocery store, and then became apprenticed to a painter and decorator. He had continued in that work for all his active life, an occupation that was to figure prominently in his other life—that of a sexually active pervert who regularly practised all the 18 perversions known to modern medicine.

At the age of 28 he had married a 19-year-old girl, by whom he had six children and, through them, had five grandchildren. After 20 years of marriage his wife absconded with their lodger, leaving Fish to raise the younger children on his own and in an empty flat from which she had previously sold all the furniture. On that score he had done well, and had stood by his children in circumstances that many normal men would have found impossible.

The dark side of Albert Fish's particular moon was horrifying. He had admitted a long series of child seductions—at least 100 in all—in which he had seduced or forced young boys into repugnant and agonizing sexual acts. When Albert Fish went out on his painting work, his overalls hid nothing but his naked flesh. Once he had cornered a child he would rip off his work-clothing and perform his unnatural acts in the nude.

## Twenty-three states

Then there was the matter of his victims. These were nearly all poor Negro children from the urban ghettoes—but sometimes they were similarly placed poor whites. Often he would pay children to bring others to him and, so Dr. Wertham estimated, his activities had spread over no fewer than 23 states of the Union. As the psychiatrist's evidence fell on the reluctant ears of the jury, each item more repulsive than the one before, it became clear, even to the prosecution, that here they were dealing with much more than the murder of a single child.

However, in the 1930s, psychiatry was less understood by the general public than it now is. It was an age of gang

**THE OBSCENE TRAGEDY took place at Wisteria Cottage (right). Fish always claimed that he had not assaulted the girl sexually—but he probably did . . .**

violence, of the anarchy of lynch law, of an administration of justice that clung firmly to the Biblical principle of an eye for an eye. For each point that Dr. Wertham raised, the prosecution produced their own expert witnesses to rebut his diagnosis that the defendant was insane.

"Tell me, Doctor, insanity is a disease of the mind, is it not?" The District Attorney remorselessly applied his legal scalpel. "If the defendant knows the difference between right and wrong, he is not insane?" Dr. Wertham was adamant. There was a world of difference between knowing right from wrong and knowing that two and two added up to four. In his opinion Fish's history spoke for itself. In no way could his actions be considered sane.

### Religious delusions

All four psychiatrists the prosecution produced agreed on one thing: Albert Fish *was* sane. The perversions he practised, they said, were practised by many others in the population. Even the eating of human excrement, one of the milder of Fish's excesses, was apparently well known among some people prominent in public life. "A quarter of the population walking the streets are psychopaths," one expert declared.

The prosecution was remorseless in its attack. At no point did it contest the facts. Yes, Albert Fish had eaten Grace Budd's flesh over a period of nine days. Yes, he had achieved a high degree of sexual stimulation through that act of cannibalism. Yes, it had been his practice to bind and castrate small boys. Yes, he did suffer from religious delusions that drove him to do these things. Nevertheless, he was still sane.

As the District Attorney summed up at the end of the trial—pouring scorn on any idea that the accused was less, or more, than an ordinary criminal—the most eloquent testimony that could have been used in his defence went unsaid. The psychiatrist who had been in charge of Fish during one of his frequent enforced stays in New York's psychiatric hospitals, and who could have given evidence as to his gross abnormality, was not called as a witness.

### A wry smile

There was little doubt about the outcome. As the jury filed back into that courtroom the foreman's face told the story. When asked for their verdict, he looked straight at the wall ahead. "Guilty of murder in the first degree." As he uttered those seven words only one person in the court remained unmoved—and that was Fish.

Throughout the trial he had acted as if it was all happening to someone else. Now, as the judge solemnly condemned

him to death by electrocution, all that Albert Fish permitted himself was a wry smile.

The reporters covering the case had decided by their own private poll that Fish was legally insane. Though the jury had brought in a different verdict, it was later revealed that most of the jurors had agreed with the defence. They had simply thought the man so crazed that a service would be done to himself, and to society, by his execution.

At the appeal, with Albert Fish already on Sing Sing's death row, Dr. Wertham repeated much of the evidence he had given to the court. The defence counsel wrung from the chief judge the admission that: "There is no doubt that this man is insane; but the question which has to be answered is, does he come within the legal definition of insanity?"

The plea that the death sentence should be commuted to one of a lifetime's confinement in an institution for the criminally insane was eventually turned down by the Court of Appeals. There was only one chance left for those who felt that to execute Fish would be legally and morally indefensible: a direct appeal to the State Governor.

### Unpunishable

On a cold January afternoon the Governor's hearing convened in a small room near his main office. The prosecution held out for the death penalty. "This is one case where I cannot see one single fact that deserves leniency on your part," the District Attorney stated. Dr. Wertham had a different view. "This man," he said, "is not only incurable and unreformable, but unpunishable. In his own distorted mind he is looking forward to the electric chair as the final experience of supreme pain." This chilling statement brought his plea to a close.

As he spoke in the eloquent voice of a man fighting for his professional principles, the legal adviser sitting at the Governor's left side seemed to nod in approval. "To execute a sick man is like burning witches," Wertham urged. "I am not appealing to you as a politician, a lawyer, or anything else—I am appealing to you as a man."

When the defence had finished its submission the Governor and his counsel rose, gave a half nod, and left the room. The plea for clemency had gone unheeded. In his Sing Sing death cell Albert Fish waited for his execution in a state of increasing excitement. On the final day Warden Lawes waited all evening in his office, hoping against hope that there

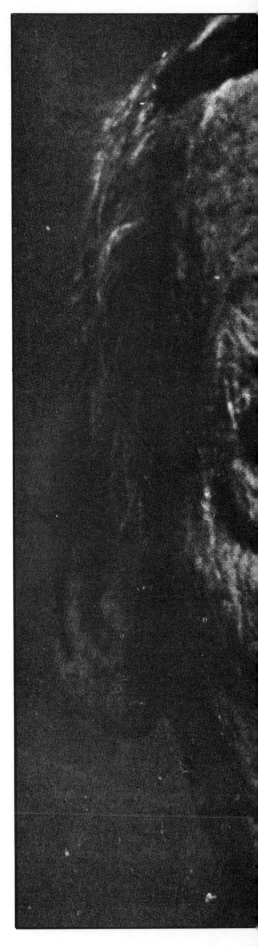

**TELL-TALE TELEGRAM . . . Experts compared the writing (inset) with that on the envelope written by Fish six years later. They decided he wrote both.**

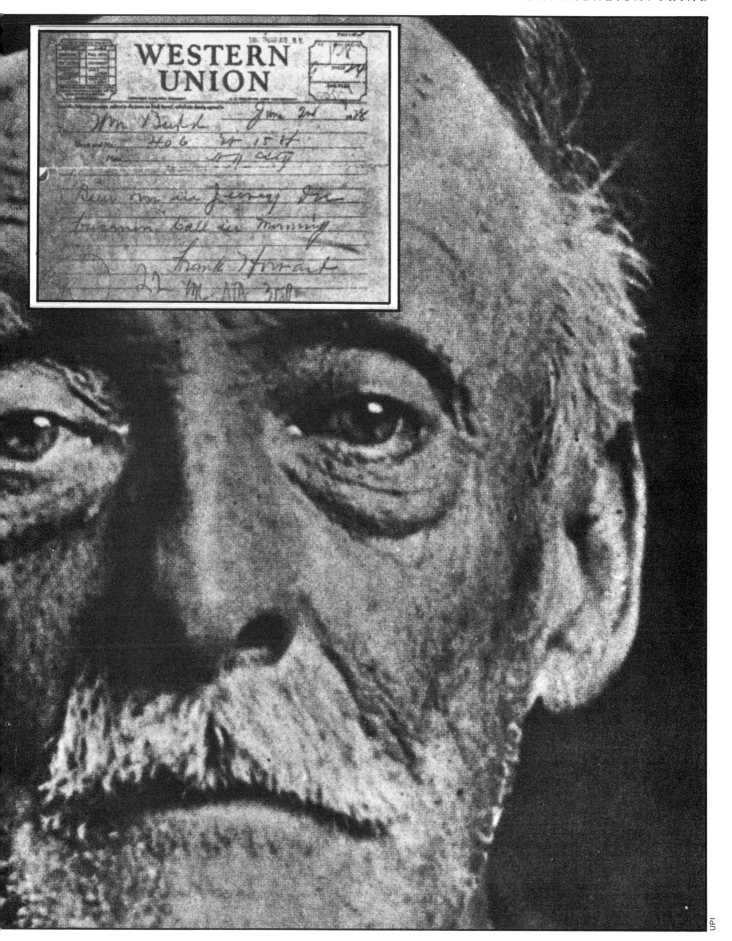

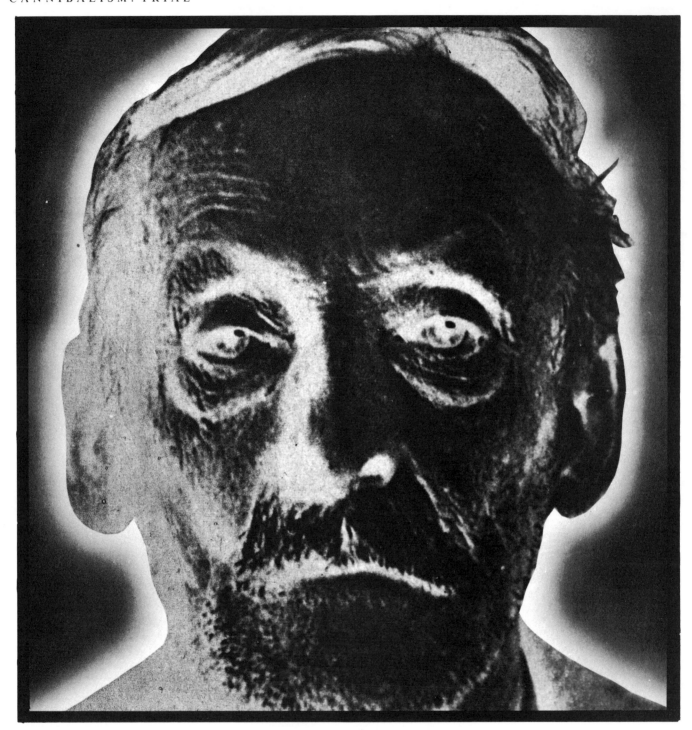

would be a reprieve from the Governor's mansion in the State capital at Albany. There was none.

As Fish was led through the door to the execution chamber he smiled benevolently at the executioner. When he was seated in the electric chair, he even helped adjust the straps and the terminals that would so shortly send him to his doom.

Shortly after nine o'clock the switch was pulled. As a reporter who was present at the execution later wrote: "Albert Fish, cannibal extraordinary, had gone the way of all flesh."

# A FEW MORTAL REMAINS

IN 1948 two schoolboys fishing for lost golf balls in a pond at Potters Bar golf links in Middlesex, England, dragged a gruesome object from the muddy water — the pelvis of a man. They had no idea what it was, so they buried it under leaves and did not bother to report their find. A few days later two other boys playing by the same pond saw a human hand and forearm in the mud. This time the boys told a group of golfers who called in the police.

It proved difficult to decide how long the remains had been immersed. The hand and forearm had been severed by rough sawing through the bone of the upper arm. The hands seemed to have been cared for during life, and the fingernails showed traces of manicuring. Fingerprint experts were called in without result. When the Thames police were ordered to drag the pond it became clear that the whole of a mutilated body was embedded in the pond.

The first two boys on the scene now came forward and pointed out where they had buried their find, and the pelvis established that the remains were those of a man. Eventually all the remains were assembled at the mortuary into an almost complete body which had been mutilated crudely with an ordinary household saw.

But how to establish the identity and age of the victim? The standard method of fixing the age of a corpse is by examining the sutures in the skull. The sutures, or thin cracks between the bones of the skull, are wide open at birth, but gradually close with advancing age until, in the 23rd year, the sutures on the top of the skull have knitted together. Those in the region of the temples join up more slowly, and seldom close very much before the 34th year.

When the tissue was removed from the skull of this victim it was seen that the top of the skull had been battered, and much of the frontal bone was missing.

105

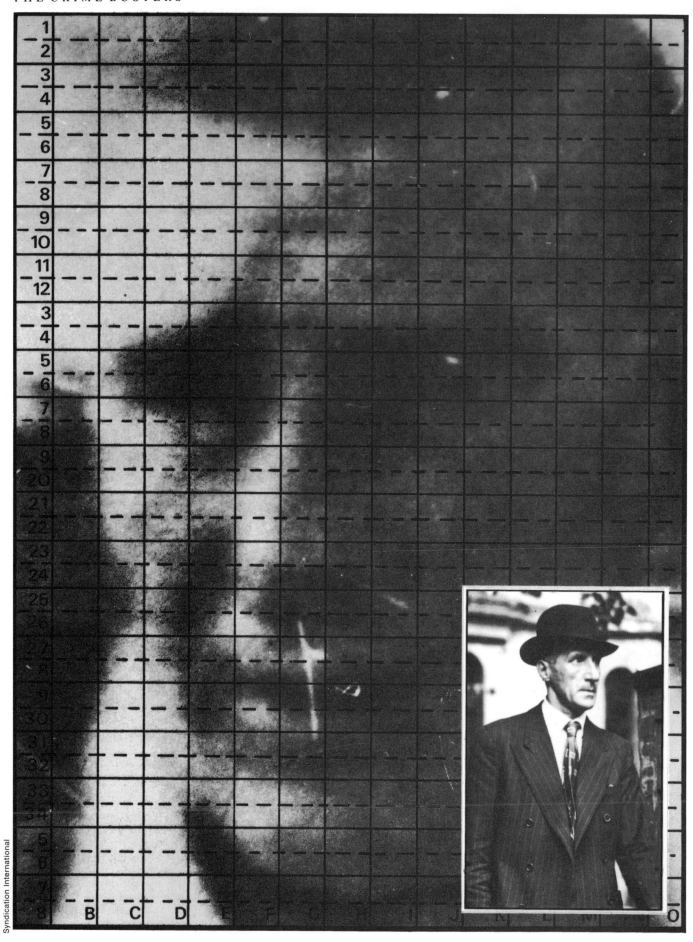

This battering had been the cause of death, a fact confirmed by injuries to the brain. The sutures at the sides of the skull had not completely knitted, although the process was well advanced. This, with certain other indications, led to the conclusion that the victim was well over 23 and probably aged between 40 and 45. Gradually the forensic scientists were building up a picture of the unknown victim. He was shown to be a slight man, well under average height, around 5 ft. 2 in., in fact. And his remains had been in the pond for at least six months.

That was the sum total of the information passed on from the pathologists to the Scotland Yard man put in charge of the case, Superintendent Colin MacDougall. This craggy, unflappable Scot started *his* search at the Yard's Missing Persons Bureau. He learned that 48 people who had been reported missing during the previous 12 months—from May 1947-48—fitted this description.

Meanwhile systematic scrutiny of the remains was going on. It was found that the lower jaw had no teeth—indeed, the sockets which once held the teeth in the lower jawbone had almost disappeared, which suggested that the victim had lost his lower teeth at least 10 years before his death. The upper jaw also had no teeth, but the teeth sockets in this case were still well defined, indicating that the victim had retained some of his own teeth, if not at death, then a very short time earlier. On the right side of the upper jaw there was a cavity in the region of the first molar. The edges of this cavity suggested that the victim had suffered from a root abscess not long before death.

Two eminent doctors were called in and helped to narrow the search for the victim's identity still further by discovering that he was left-handed—this was established by careful comparison and measurement of the left and right clavicles and scapulae. (The clavicle is the collar-bone and the scapulae the shoulder-blades.)

Now, of the 48 missing men on MacDougall's list only two were known to have been left-handed, and one of the two had a deformation of the little finger of the left hand, which eliminated him, leaving only one possibility: Albert Welch, a railway worker aged 44, who had been reported missing the previous October. What clinched the identification was that Welch had lived in Potters Bar.

MacDougall had now to set about the remorseless build-up of detail which, although unexciting in detective fiction,

**SHEER PERSISTENCE on the part of Superintendent MacDougall (left inset) produced an identification of the victim. Above right: Welch in happier days with his wife, and (below) his delayed funeral.**

Syndication International

Associated Newspapers

is the foundation of all successful police work. First MacDougall had to trace the dentist who had treated Welch. This took time, as the dentist had retired and destroyed his records. However, he remembered removing Welch's lower teeth many years before and fitting a full lower denture. The next step was to find a photograph of Welch. MacDougall came up with a holiday snap but could get no information about the camera which took it.

The skull was then carefully reconstructed and the lower jaw set in its true anatomical position by using dental articulators and making dentures to fit the jaw. The whole was then photographed and the print enlarged to life-size. The snapshot was also enlarged to life-size, a toy bucket which appeared in the background of the original being used as a standard of scale. This enlargement was printed on a transparency and superimposed over a life-size photograph of the rebuilt skull.

The superimposition was a perfect job; the pathologist had noticed that the thin bone which divides the nostrils of the skull—the septum—was deformed and,

since the sinuses were also malformed, it was more than likely that the victim had suffered from sinus trouble. The superimposed snapshot and skull photographs matched precisely where the septum was deformed.

Armed with all this knowledge, Superintendent MacDougall interviewed Welch's workmates and learned that Welch had complained of severe toothache not long before he was reported missing. Another remembered that the man had suffered from chronic catarrh, and all his mates had noticed what care he had taken of his hands and fingernails. One puzzling feature of the pathologist's report took some time to work out—the unusually well-preserved muscle tissue of Welch's knees. At last it dawned on the investigators that the man's job as a railway signal linesman meant that much of his work had to be done in a kneeling position.

**GRIM AFFAIR . . . Mrs. Welch (inset) refused to attend the funeral of her murdered husband. She could not believe that the police had truly identified him.**

Still MacDougall felt that the picture of the missing man so far was not complete enough to satisfy a jury. He needed a stroke of luck, and he got it. A detective scouring an allotment shed owned by Welch produced a pair of the man's boots. Casts made from glycerine-gelatine and formalin were prepared, and these clearly showed the outline of Welch's foot—and that he must have had stiff big-toe joints. The feet from the pond were X-rayed, and there were unmistakable signs of stiffening of the big-toe joints. When the X-ray negatives were superimposed over the internal impressions of the boots there was complete agreement.

At last MacDougall felt that he had pieced together enough of the jig-saw to lay the facts before the Hendon coroner, Dr. Cogswell, who sat with a jury and returned a verdict that the remains were those of Albert Welch. It was a triumph of co-operation between police and forensic scientists.

Alas, the man who killed Albert Welch got clean away with the murder. He was never brought to book.

Mary Evans

# TERROR BY GASLIGHT

The seedy night-life of nineteenth-century cities was replete with violence, disease and death. It was the heyday of freaks and monsters whose means of livelihood was to sell passers-by a glimpse of their distorted limbs — and of conmen and crooks ready to murder for the price of a cheap meal . . .

ONE cold, foggy evening in the late 1860s Sir Frederick Treves, a surgeon at the Mile End Infirmary in east London, was walking home along the Whitechapel Road. Hansom cabs clattered by on the wet cobbles, and Sir Frederick had to walk cautiously to avoid cracks in the pavement. Perhaps this was why he noticed a strip of canvas flapping in the cold wind. By the dim gaslight he could just make out the words: "Elephant Man — admission twopence."

He pushed aside a greasy canvas flap and found himself in a narrow space between two buildings. In Victorian times these were known as "holes in the wall": space was so valuable in the overcrowded slums that the gaps between houses were covered with a canvas roof and let out at low rents. There was a single dim light, and the surgeon could see a huddled figure, covered in tarpaulin, and sitting on a packing case. The surgeon gently pulled back the tarpaulin, and the man

**LYING IN WAIT . . . Unsuspecting citizens foolish enough to walk alone at night in the streets of London were easy meat for the legion of prowling thieves.**

looked up at him. What Sir Frederick saw made him gasp. The "elephant man's" face was hardly human; the nose was a swollen, trunk-like mass of flesh, and everything else about him was distorted.

The surgeon drew up a packing case, and sat talking to this human creature who looked like a beast from a fairy tale. The elephant man proved to be a man of mystery. His body was as distorted as his face, so it was not even clear to which sex "he" belonged. He knew that his name was John Merrick and that he was about 20. But he could only speak in an incomprehensible mumble, and could apparently remember nothing of his origins, or where he had grown up. When his "keepers" came back from the pub, where they had been drinking to keep out

the cold, they told Treves that they had simply found the elephant man wandering in the street, and had decided that he might bring them in a few pence as a freak show. But he was so horrible that women fainted at the sight of him and children had fits.

When the surgeon offered them five pounds for the monster, they could scarcely believe their luck. The next day Treves took the elephant man to the hospital, and gave him a private suite of rooms, cut off from the rest of the building. Few nurses could bear to see him, and before a nurse was asked to bring him food or help him to dress she was given a preliminary look at him to see if she could bear it without fainting.

Yet the elephant man proved to be gentle and charming. His gratitude touched everybody. Obviously, his life had been hard and miserable; no one had ever been kind to him. Now, at last, he had warmth and comfort, and he found it almost impossible to believe that fate had finally relented towards him.

One of his favourite occupations was cutting pictures out of illustrated magazines. One of these—his most treasured—was of Princess Alexandra, who would be Queen of England when her husband, later Edward VII, came to the throne. The princess was the patroness of the hospital, and she was deeply interested in the elephant man. One day she told Treves she wanted to see him. Treves tried hard to dissuade her, but she was determined. She was shown into the elephant man's presence. She did not flinch as the twisted, monstrous creature dragged himself towards her, or as he took her hand in his own distorted claw and bent over to kiss it. Then she was shown out. As the door closed behind her, she fainted.

This strange story of the pathetic human monstrosity involves no crime, yet it is thoroughly typical of that foggy, gaslit London that was drawn so powerfully by the artist Gustave Doré. It was a grim city in which mothers with babies at their breast slept out on the freezing pavements, a city of disease, violence and corruption. It comes to life in the pages of that curious work called *My Secret Life* by an unknown Victorian whom we know only as Walter. Walter often wandered around the slum streets, seeking to satisfy his peculiar desires.

He might have a sudden impulse to have sex with a pregnant woman, or with a young virgin, or even a child. On one occasion he picked up a woman and a 10-year-old girl, went back to a cold, dismal room with them and spent the night possessing them both. Moreover, it was not the first time the child had been made to give herself to a man for money. Again and again Walter describes buying young girls for a shilling.

**Coarse-looking**

It was a city of unsolved mystery. The Jack the Ripper murders are the most famous of these; but there are many others that are equally strange. For example, there was the case of the disappearing German baker. His name was Urban Napoleon Stanger, and he and his wife were natives of Kreuznach, in Germany. They bought a house at 136 Lever Street, behind Gray's Inn Road.

It was a rough area, which had been the scene of many crimes, and Pentonville Prison was not far away. However, it was densely populated, and Stanger's bakery business prospered. There were many Germans living in the area—mostly of Jewish extraction. Stanger became friendly with another baker called Felix Strumm. Strumm had a dark beard, a hooked nose, dark, deep-set eyes and a powerful body; he gave an impression of

Mary Evans

cunning and malice, but Stanger seemed to like him. So did Mrs. Stanger, a hard-faced, coarse-looking woman.

On the evening of November 12, 1881, Stanger's journeyman baker walked past the shop around midnight and saw Stanger, Strumm and two other men talking outside the shop; then Stanger went inside. He was never seen again. When the journeyman got to the shop the next day, Mrs. Stanger immediately sent him to get Strumm, who lived nearby. He came, and stayed all day. Two people who came to see Stanger were told he had gone to Germany on business.

Elizabeth Stanger and Strumm began to be seen in public together, usually arm in arm. And a few weeks later residents of Lever Street were amazed when they saw Strumm painting out the name of Stanger from above the shop and substituting his own. Rumour went around that Mrs. Stanger had found an interesting way of disposing of her husband: converting him into meat pies. The sale of their meat pies dropped, but otherwise business continued to prosper. The police decided there were no grounds for taking action, even though several neighbours talked about Stanger's disappearance.

In April 1882, six months after the baker's disappearance, an advertisement appeared in the press offering a £50

POLICE made some effort to control the burgeoning crime wave which, at one time, threatened to engulf Britain's cities. Eventually they succeeded . . .

reward for anyone who could give information leading to the discovery of the whereabouts of Stanger. It seems to have been inserted by a relative of Stanger's who was not satisfied with Mrs. Stanger's story about the sudden visit to Germany.

Finally Stanger's solicitors brought a charge against Strumm, accusing him of forging a cheque in Stanger's name. Strumm and Mrs. Stanger were both detained. In court Mrs. Stanger was shrill, Strumm was sullen, both were defiant. Their story was that Stanger had been a spendthrift and was heavily in debt. The virtuous Strumm often lent him money. One day, after Mrs. Stanger had taxed her husband with his feckless ways, Stanger announced he was going to leave her. Mrs. Stanger went to bed in tears, and next morning her husband had gone. Since then, she said, Strumm had helped her run the business.

It was all manifestly untrue. Stanger had nearly £500 in the bank when he disappeared, and Strumm had been out of work and in debt before he moved into the bakery in Lever Street. Stanger's will deepened the suspicion that he had been murdered. He left his money to his wife – on condition she did not marry or live with another man. This suggested he suspected her of being involved with Strumm – something the whole neighbourhood had known in any case.

Mrs. Stanger was questioned as a witness and made a bad impression; she was hooted and hissed as she left court. When the jury announced a verdict of guilty, Strumm stood up and bellowed with rage. The judge, perhaps irritated by this display of contempt of court, sentenced him to the maximum for forgery – 10 years. Strumm proved to be a bad prisoner, violent and resentful, and he served the whole term. Mrs. Stanger, surrounded by hostile neighbours, returned to Germany – in the company of Mrs. Strumm, it is said.

It seems fairly certain that Mrs. Stanger murdered her husband that night in November, and that she sent for Strumm to help her dispose of the body. But how she killed him, and what became

—Mansell

**HORRIFYING FREAKS were a source of great entertainment even to "respectable ladies" . . . Above: One of Gustave Doré's versions of a low-life London tea-bar.**

of the body, will never be known. Strumm's rage was undoubtedly due to a sense of the sheer unfairness of it. *He* had not killed Stanger; his mistress had. He had only forged a cheque. Yet it would have done him no good to denounce her to the court; the result would only be that she would probably hang, and he would get another 10 years added to his sentence as an accessory. Hence, one presumes, his baffled rage.

Two other unsolved murders created a great deal of public excitement. One of

these became known as the Euston Square Mystery. One day in 1879 a man named Severin Bastendorf brought in some workmen to help him clear rubbish out of his cellar at 4 Euston Square, so that he could use it for storing coal. Under a pile of old refuse they found the skeleton of a woman, with a piece of rope around the neck. Bloodstains on the floor suggested she had been stabbed as well as strangled. The woman had suffered from curvature of the spine, and this made it easy to identify her.

She had been a lodger of the Bastendorfs, and her name was Matilda Hacker. She was a strange, eccentric woman with golden curls, who dressed like a teenage beauty, although she was approaching middle age. She apparently came from a wealthy Canterbury family, but one of her eccentricities was to skip from lodging to lodging to avoid her creditors. She had vanished 18 months before, and a maidservant named Hannah Dobbs announced that the eccentric lady had done another moonlight flit. Shortly thereafter Hannah Dobbs herself had left.

### No evidence

Hannah Dobbs was the obvious suspect. And this view was confirmed when the police traced a gold watch belonging to Miss Hacker to a pawnbroker, and learned that it had been pawned by a woman answering to Hannah's description. She was located in prison, where she was serving six months for theft, and put on trial. But since there was no definite evidence against her she was acquitted. Some time afterwards a pamphlet was published, apparently written by Hannah Dobbs.

She claimed that the murder of Miss Hacker had been committed by her lover,

the younger brother of Severin Bastendorf. She said that she had only helped conceal the body. This could be the solution of the "Euston Square Mystery", yet why should Hannah Dobbs want to denounce her lover, and implicate herself as an accessory, after her acquittal?

### Bad reputation

Equally baffling was the murder of Mrs. Sarah Millsom. On Wednesday, April 11, 1866, Mrs. Millsom, a housekeeper who lived at 3 Cannon Street in the City of London, was sitting in her room reading, while the cook, Elizabeth Lowes, sat sewing opposite. Just after nine in the evening there was a ring at the doorbell. Mrs. Millsom jumped up. "That's for me." She went downstairs. After a while the cook wondered what had happened to her; she lit a candle and went downstairs.

Mrs. Millsom lay dead at the bottom of the stairs, her face and head a mass of blood. Someone had battered her to death. There had been no robbery – her keys were untouched – and the motive was not sexual, for her clothes were undisturbed. It was found that she had borrowed money from a moneylender to pass on to a man called George Terry. But Terry had been in the poorhouse at the time of the murder. A friend of Terry's with a bad reputation, a man named Smith, was charged with the murder, but was able to establish a perfect alibi. And the police were never able to discover why a highly respectable housekeeper should rush downstairs, obviously expecting a man, but meet a violent death.

But perhaps the strangest of all the insoluble mysteries of Victorian London was the series of disappearances that have become known simply as the

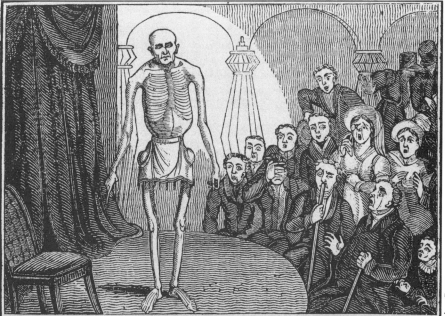
Mary Evans

"vanishings". They began in 1881, and centred around the areas of East Ham and West Ham. Because these disappearances were unsolved, there is no complete account of them. An 11-year-old girl named Eliza Carter left home one day wearing a blue dress with buttons down the front. A few hours later she was seen by a friend, and seemed to be in a state of terror. For some odd reason, she said she didn't dare to go home. Then she simply vanished.

The blue dress was found on the East Ham football ground—minus all its buttons. Eliza was never seen again. Charles Wagner, the son of a West Ham butcher, vanished one day, and his body was later found at the foot of cliffs at Ramsgate, 75 miles away. The odd thing was that it was not a fall that had caused death, neither was he drowned. The body bore no signs of injury, and there was no obvious cause of death.

### Flying saucers

In January 1890 three girls vanished together from West Ham. Only one of them—15-year-old Amelia Jeffs—was found in West Ham Park; she had been strangled after a violent struggle. But the "vanishings"—a dozen or more—had finished. A woman had been seen talking to the three girls just before their disappearance. Seven years earlier an old woman had been speaking to Eliza Carter just before she vanished. The coroner who examined Amelia Jeffs remarked "women are as susceptible to the lowest forms of mania as men".

Presumably he was hinting at sadistic sexual perversion—probably with the Ripper in mind—the Ripper murders had all taken place in the second half of 1888, and had ceased after the disembowelling of Mary Kelly on November 8th. But the bodies of the Ripper's victims were always left lying where he killed them.

What was the coroner hinting at? That the vanished children had been kidnapped, and perhaps maltreated until they died? If so, why. was Charles Wagner's body free of injury? No doubt there are modern speculators in the field of the "occult" who would favour the theory that the children were snatched up by flying saucers. It has to be admitted that this explanation is just about as likely as any other. The "vanishings" remain one of the most disturbing mysteries of the age.

### Disgusting flesh

But it would be a mistake to convey the impression that the most famous crimes of the age were all confined to London. Charlie Peace pursued his burglarious profession in Sheffield; Dr. Pritchard poisoned his wife and mother-in-law in Glasgow; Constance Kent almost decapitated her four-year-old brother at

Rode, in Somerset; and America's classic "crime of the century"—Professor Webster's murder of his colleague Dr. Parkman—took place in the Boston Medical College. And in the 1870s it was enough to mention the name "Sheward" to make Victorian ladies grow pale and reach for their smelling salts. The case, which has now been almost forgotten, caused something like hysteria at the time.

It began, as far as the general public was concerned, on a Saturday evening, June 21, 1851, when a dwarf named Charles Johnson took his dog for a walk in the countryside near Norwich. The dog vanished behind a hedge and reappeared with a disgusting lump of flesh in its teeth. It was only when they got home that Johnson realized it was a human hand.

The police were called, and more pieces

PUNCH, OR THE LONDON CHARIVARI.—September 29, 1888.

## THE NEMESIS OF NEGLECT.

"THERE FLOATS A PHANTOM ON THE SLUM'S FOUL AIR,
SHAPING, TO EYES WHICH HAVE THE GIFT OF SEEING,
INTO THE SPECTRE OF THAT LOATHLY LAIR.
FACE IT—FOR VAIN IS FLEEING!
RED-HANDED, RUTHLESS, FURTIVE, UNERECT,
'TIS MURDEROUS CRIME—THE NEMESIS OF NEGLECT!"

Both Mary Evans

SMOGBOUND, filthy and overcrowded, London was, in Victorian times, the most crime-ridden city in the world. Slums proliferated, as Doré noted (above), and casual murder was so common that *Punch* felt perfectly justified in publishing cartoons on the subject (left). England was the first country to suffer from the now all-too-well-known results of the Industrial Revolution, when thousands flocked to the towns from the countryside in search of non-existent riches.

of flesh were found in the field. The following day a female pelvis was found nearby. Doctors announced that the remains were those of a teenage girl, who had been dead about a fortnight. And since Victorian newspaper readers were just as prone to jump to conclusions as those of today, the case immediately excited a universal morbid excitement. It seemed horribly probable there was a sex maniac loose in the Norwich area.

More pieces of the body continued to turn up: in ditches, sewers, fields. It was as if the murderer had embarked on some gruesome cross-country chase, scattering clues behind him. When a left foot was discovered in a churchyard, and the left hand was found nearby — with the ring finger missing — the whole of East Anglia talked of nothing but the mystery. Relatives of a missing servant girl named Ann Bailey were certain that she had been murdered by a man named Gouch, with whom she had eloped.

### Haggard-looking

When Ann Bailey turned up safe and sound the police seemed to become discouraged. It seemed incredible that no one had observed the disappearance of a young girl from the area. But as the months drifted by it seemed clear that no one had. And finally the Norwich mystery went into the "unsolved" file.

A part of the body was preserved in spirits of wine at the local Guildhall — it looked as though it were boiled.

Seventeen years passed. On New Year's Day, 1869, a bearded, haggard-looking man walked into the police station at Walworth, south London, and said he wanted to confess to a murder. He gave his name as William Sheward, and said that for the past two days he had been trying to work up the nerve to commit suicide. Unable to do it, he had decided to give himself up. The murder, he said, had taken place in Norwich in 1851; the victim had been his 56-year-old wife.

### Highly sexed

Now, at last, it was clear how Sheward had got away with it for so long. Although many relatives had enquired after Mrs. Sheward, and been suspicious of her disappearance, no one thought of connecting it with the remains of a "teenage" girl.

The story that emerged in Sheward's confession was of a thoroughly unhappy marriage. He was an unsuccessful tailor. At the age of 24 — in 1836 — he had married his 39-year-old housekeeper, Martha Francis. They quarrelled a great deal; Sheward began to drink as his business failed. He and his wife had never been sexually compatible; he was highly sexed, and she was not. On June 15, 1851, they quarrelled about money.

Sheward lost his temper, seized a razor and "ran it into her throat". This took place in the bedroom. The next day the corpse began to smell, so Sheward began to hack it up. He took some pieces in a bag and threw them away on a country walk. The next day he continued the mutilation, boiling the head in a saucepan to stop it from smelling.

### Gruesome deed

It took him all week, during which time anyone walking into the house — while he was at work — could have solved the mystery of the hands and feet that were now being picked up around Norwich. He ended, the following weekend, by burning the sheets and blankets. From then on, he told relatives that Mrs. Sheward had gone to New Zealand. Not long after he met a younger woman, who lived with him and bore him several children. But the memory of his gruesome deed haunted him, giving him no peace, until he suddenly decided to end it all by killing himself. . . .

The jury found him guilty, with no extenuating circumstances — no doubt influenced by the horror of the crime; Sheward was executed in April 1869.

The age of gaslight was not all horror: there was Sherlock Holmes and Gilbert and Sullivan, as well as Jack the Ripper and William Sheward. But on the whole it leaves no cause for nostalgia or regret.

CHARLES PEACE.

114

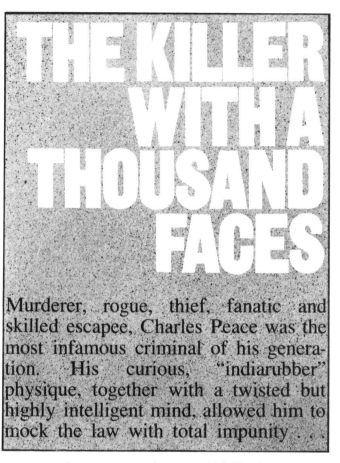

# THE KILLER WITH A THOUSAND FACES

Murderer, rogue, thief, fanatic and skilled escapee, Charles Peace was the most infamous criminal of his generation. His curious, "indiarubber" physique, together with a twisted but highly intelligent mind, allowed him to mock the law with total impunity . . .

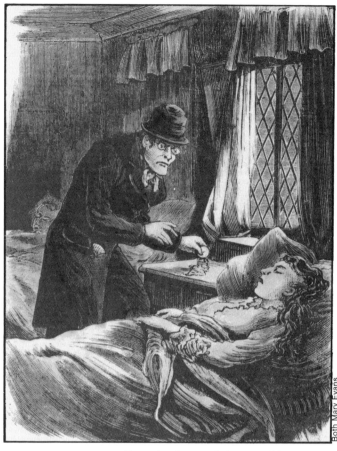

Both Mary Evans

THE new prisoner was certainly an odd specimen. For a start, he could change the shape of his face as if it were putty.

John Ward, he called himself. "Complexion dark, clean-shaven, hair grey, eyes hazel, one darker than the other, large mouth, long scar on side of left leg and back of thigh, forefinger of left hand missing, address unknown." That was how he had been described by the Duty Sergeant on the day he had been arrested.

Any description would have fitted equally well. The man had a thousand faces. He even played a little game with the warders. "Hey, young fellow!" he would call to one of the officers, sticking his head through the grille of his cell door. "Take a good look!" His head would pop back in like a tortoise, then reappear with every feature twisted out of recognition; his jaw mis-shapen, his eyebrows hidden in the folds of his forehead, his mouth champing like a monkey.

## Pious moralizing

It was a grotesque sight. "Now then, officer," he would cackle. "Could you describe me to a judge now? As an honest man, could you?"

There was another strange thing about Mr. Ward's appearance. At first, his complexion had been unusually dark—"negroid", one policeman had described it. Now it was becoming lighter.

Everything about the mysterious Mr.

Ward was a contradiction. When he wasn't contorting his face into hideous grimaces, he looked like a frail and doddery old man, with white hair, bowed shoulders and a faltering step. Yet, undressed, he had the physique of a man 20 years younger, lithe, muscular and agile.

His arrest after shooting and wounding a policeman had shocked everyone who knew him, though they were puzzled why the upright citizen they knew as John Thompson should have called himself John Ward. Mr. Thompson was respected by all his neighbours as a sober and God-fearing man, devoted equally to pious moralizing and amateur home-music-making. The residents of Peckham, a sedate and suffocatingly respectable suburb of south-east London, were sure there had been a mistake. But Police-constable R202 Edward Robinson had a shattered arm to prove his story.

The riddle was, if the "indiarubber man" had been leading a double life and was neither John Ward nor John Thompson, then who was he?

One by one, police chiefs from all over London filed past Ward's cell in Newgate Jail, hoping to recognize him. The man was highly indignant. "You've never set eyes on me!" he said. "I've never been in a place like this before!"

Mr. Ward was still protesting angrily when a woman called Mrs. Sue Thompson called at the jail and asked to see the two

officers in charge of the case. She seemed nervous and distraught. "I understand there's a possibility of a reward," she said hesitantly. "I mean, for the man you have here who calls himself John Ward. We've been living together under the name of Thompson . . ."

The officers smiled patiently. "There must be a mistake," said one. "There's no reward for anyone called either Ward or Thompson."

## Gaslit streets

"You don't understand," said Mrs. Thompson. "His real name is Peace. Charles Peace."

The smiles faded from the officers' faces. "Good god!" exclaimed Inspector John Bonney. "We've got Charlie Peace!"

The name screamed from "WANTED" posters all over Britain. Murderer, thief, burglar, pickpocket, Charlie Peace had been a one-man crime wave for nearly 30 years. His exploits had become a living legend. He was the man who boasted that no detective was clever enough to catch him, who had slipped through the fingers of the Law a thousand times, whose adventures were followed by the public as if he were some modern Robin Hood.

The greatest criminal who ever haunted the foggy and gaslit streets of Britain had been behind bars for three weeks, and they hadn't even realized it. All they had to do now was hang on to him. Elated

115

though they were by their accidental success, Inspector Bonney and Inspector Philips were only too aware that their problems had only just started, for Charlie Peace had one other headline-making ability. He was a virtuoso escape artist, who could squeeze through a space six inches wide, pad across rooftops like a cat, somersault over a brick wall, and who claimed, "I'm more than a match for any three men."

Charlie Peace was really half-a-dozen men rolled into one. He could have made a living—and occasionally did—as a violinist, an entertainer, an acrobat, an actor, a carpenter or an antique-dealer. But some perverse streak in his nature, hardened by the social conditions of the time, led him to crime.

### Tiny footprints

He was ugly, yet he had a strange power over women. He was violent, yet loved animals and children. He was merciless to those who crossed him, yet he could pray for hours on end and talk theology to a Bishop. He was outstandingly quick-witted and intelligent, yet there were those who called him insane.

Whether Charlie Peace was crippled in mind, nobody will ever know. He was certainly crippled in body. With the inhumanity that lurked beneath the self-righteous patina of Victorian society, Charlie Peace had been sent to work in a

**HARD BARGAINER . . . Peace was, of course, also an expert in the disposal of stolen goods. Right: The house in Peckham where Charlie lived in 1877 . . .**

steel mill at 13, tending machines that were lethally dangerous. One day, a length of white-hot steel shot out of his machine and went right through his leg, just above the kneebone. The machine had to be put into reverse before the rod could be removed, and he was maimed for life. His career of crime started the day he left hospital on crutches, branded as incurable and thrown onto a labour market that had no room for cripples.

With bravery and determination, helped by an incredibly tough physique, Charlie Peace overcame his disability to such an extent that he could perform as an acrobat and tumbler. His strength was known and feared throughout his home town of Sheffield. He once picked up a ferocious bulldog by its lower jaw and beat it into insensibility with his other hand.

But there was another, more sensitive side to his character. He learned the violin and had such an instinctive feeling for the instrument that he was able to tour the countryside, playing at fairs and dances. He joined a troupe of actors, performing sketches and excerpts from Shakespeare. Walking home one night, still in his theatrical make-up, he realized that nobody could recognize him. This

discovery inspired a series of disguises which were to fool the police and earn him the title of "The man with the india-rubber face". For he had already started on the road that would lead to the gallows.

High above the damp and dimly lit streets, Charlie Peace went to work each night with his violin-case. It contained no instrument, but a complete set of housebreaking tools. The "fiddler on the roof" was a cat-burglar. He was so deft and agile that he could ransack six houses in one night, moving swiftly and silently from roof to roof in stockinged feet. In the morning the only clues were a series of tiny, indistinct footprints on the tiles—so small that for a long time it was thought Charlie Peace was a child.

He used every skill he possessed. His father had been an animal-trainer, and Charlie Peace had inherited his understanding of animals. Only now he applied it to watchdogs. The most homicidal mastiffs ended up licking his fingers and accepting the drugged meat he always carried. Time and again the extraordinary suppleness of his acrobat's body saved him from capture. Surprised one night by a householder, he wound himself clear of the ground round the leg of a single-leg dining-table, hidden from view by an overhanging tablecloth. The man looked around, shrugged his shoulders and went back to bed. Peace screwed up the doors of the room to prevent being disturbed

Mary Evans. Radio Times

again and continued sorting out the loot.

Things didn't always go smoothly and silently. By 1872 he had been jailed four times and spent more than 15 years behind bars, but each time he emerged more cunning and desperate than before. He had learned to alter his features at will, so that every identification photograph seemed to show a different man. He darkened his face with walnut juice. He also started carrying a revolver, strapped to his wrist. Experimenting with various types of cartridges one day, he blew off his left forefinger. Even then, he put the injury to good use. He invented a false arm with a hook at the end, which both concealed his telltale hand and provided a useful disguise.

This theatrical skill frequently got him out of trouble. The headmaster of an exclusive boys' school was delighted when a dignified-looking old man called and offered to entertain the pupils with a few hours with songs, recitations and scenes from Shakespeare. The performance was a resounding success. The Gravedigger's Scene from *Hamlet* brought the house down, and even the masters were entranced by the man's ability to play tunes on a one-string fiddle made out of an ordinary walking-stick. The "all-round entertainer" didn't leave until darkness fell and it was safe to step outside. It was Charlie Peace. What the headmaster didn't know was

**HE WAS UGLY (left), but nonetheless successful with women. In fact he was already a legendary figure by the time he finally fell into the hands of police.**

that he had been on the run from the police — and the school was the safest place to hide out.

The sparse and slow-moving police force — Britain had only just progressed from centuries of night-watchmen and "voluntary constables" — was no match for Charlie Peace. He once stopped at one of his own "Wanted" posters and asked a policeman, "Have they found that scoundrel Peace yet?" When police searched a train, acting on a tip-off that Peace was among the passengers, they were reinforced by an excitable old man with white hair, who ran up and down the carriages babbling, "Come out, you rascal! You can't escape!" It was Charlie Peace again.

**Lunatic obsession**

In 1875, Peace moved to the village of Darnall with his long-suffering wife, Hannah, and stepson, Willie. Unfortunately for Peace a new vicar moved in the same week. It was the Rev. J. H. Littlewood, Peace's former chaplain at Wakefield Jail. The two men met face to face in the High Street. Peace forced his features into a deferential smile and raised his hat. That evening, Peace called

on the vicar and pleaded with him not to give away his identity. "Have mercy on me and my family," he begged. "I've completely reformed. I'm going straight and trying to build a new life." The parson agreed to keep Peace's secret — provided he went to church every Sunday and behaved like an honest and pious citizen.

Nobody could outdo Charlie Peace when it came to praising the Lord, and he fully lived up to the parson's confidence. He was on his knees faster and delivered his "Amens" more fervently than any other member of the congregation. Soon he was conducting the children's Bible classes. As a token of his esteem, he presented Mr. Littlewood with an ingenious mechanical singing bird, forgetting to add the fact that it had been stolen from a wealthy collector in another county.

It was "The Case of the Sunday School Clock" that eventually caused the vicar to fall out with his plausible new parishioner. Mr. Littlewood noticed it was missing and immediately suspected Peace. Peace hotly denied the accusations, but things were never the same again. Many years later, the trivial, parish-pump affair was to have an extraordinary sequel.

But now Peace had a bigger problem on his mind; a problem fated to spiral into a lunatic obsession which was to rob him of all sense of caution. He had fallen in love with his next-door

Mary Evans

neighbour, Mrs. Katherine Dyson, who lived with her husband, Arthur, a 6 ft. 5 ins. but docile railroad engineer. Peace wormed his way into the Dysons' home, and, at first, Mrs. Dyson responded to his advances, meeting him secretly in the attic which linked the two houses.

Then she made her fatal mistake. She told Peace she was tired of him and didn't wish to see him any more. Peace refused to take no for an answer. He bombarded Mrs. Dyson with calls and letters, and gradually his infatuation with Mrs. Dyson soured and twisted into a form of persecution. He peered through the couple's windows at night, shouted abuse at them in the street, followed them round the village muttering threats. It was too much even for the quiet and retiring Mr. Dyson, a gentle giant of a man. In a stiff and futile gesture, he threw his visiting card into Peace's garden, bearing the message, "Charles Peace is requested not to interfere with my family."

The action only inflamed Peace further. He became almost demented. "He had a way of creeping and crawling about and coming upon you suddenly unawares," recalled Mrs. Dyson. "I cannot describe to you how he seemed to wriggle himself inside a door, or the terrible expression on his face. He seemed more like an evil spirit than a man. I used to be especially afraid of him at nights because he had a

**CAPTURED AT LAST! P.C. Robinson bravely struggles with Peace and succeeds in overpowering him. In jail (right) the prisoner was the object of much interest.**

habit of continually prowling about the house and turning up suddenly. He would, too, assume all sorts of disguises. He used to boast how effectively he could disguise himself. He once said, 'I am never beaten when I have made up my mind. If I make up my mind to a thing, I am bound to have it, even if it costs me my life'." In the end it did just that.

On the evening of July 1, 1875, Mrs. Dyson was gossiping with some neighbours outside her house. Without a sound, Peace emerged from the shadows and walked up to her. His eyes were wild and his manner agitated. He pulled a revolver from his pocket, pointed it at her head and threatened, "I'll blow your bloody brains out and your bloody husband's, too." The threat misfired. Far from terrorizing the Dysons, it made up their minds. They took him to court.

An appearance before a magistrate — where awkward questions might be asked — was a risk Peace couldn't take. He failed to answer the summons, and a warrant was issued for his arrest. The Dysons heaved a sigh of relief. Their tormentor had gone. . . or so they thought. The only reminder of the unpleasant incident was a few letters in the post,

some abusive, others pleading for Mrs. Dyson to withdraw the summons.

Just before midnight, exactly one month later, 20-year-old Police-constable Nicholas Cock left a police-station in Manchester to patrol his regular beat. He seemed disturbed. "I've got a feeling something dreadful is going to happen tonight," he told his friends.

**Paroxysm of hate**

About 30 minutes later he noticed a suspicious figure lurking round a large, detached house in Seymour Grove. While P.C. Beanland, who had been patrolling nearby, crept up the drive, P.C. Cock positioned himself behind a rear wall to catch the intruder if he tried to escape through the back. As P.C. Beanland's bullseye lantern flickered over the front of the house, a figure detached itself from the bushes and sped down the garden, vaulting the wall in one leap. He landed almost in P.C. Cock's arms.

"Stand back, or I'll shoot," said the man, producing a revolver from his sleeve. Courageously, P.C. Cock reached for his truncheon and moved forward. The man fired one shot wide, but the constable kept on coming. The next shot hit him full in the chest. He fell, groaning, "Oh, murder, murder, I'm shot, I'm shot." P.C. Beanland raced to his aid, but the young policeman was already dying. "Who shot you?" asked P.C. Beanland

Radio Times

urgently. "I don't know," gasped P.C. Cock. They were his last words.

He was right. In the darkness, few people could have recognized the wild and distorted face of Charlie Peace. Either way, it made little difference, for the police already had a suspect. A few days earlier, three young Irishmen—the Habron brothers—had threatened to shoot P.C. Cock. That night, Police-Superintendent William Bent led a raid on the shack the three brothers used as a home.

The men were hauled from their beds and charged with the murder of P.C. Cock. The circumstantial evidence against them constituted a formidable case. There was the threat overheard by several witnesses. There had been mud on their boots. Their alibi that they had been in bed two hours before the murder was not substantiated by a local publican, who remembered them drinking until 11 p.m.

On November 27, 23-year-old John Habron and his 18-year-old brother, William, stood trial at Manchester Assizes, both knowing they were completely innocent. The jury took $2\frac{1}{2}$ hours to consider its verdict. John was found Not Guilty. William was Guilty, and condemned to death.

In the public gallery, one man seemed particularly satisfied with the verdict. It was Charlie Peace, who had slipped into the court to see injustice done. But

**ARRAIGNED by the chief magistrate (above), Charlie protested his innocence to the charge of attempted murder and firmly maintained his false identity . . .**

William Habron did not hang; just before the date set for his execution, the Home Secretary issued a reprieve, and his sentence was commuted to 20 years' penal servitude in Portland Prison.

Peace had ducked out of one noose, only to place his head in another. For the day after Habron had been sentenced to death for the crime he had committed, Peace murdered the inoffensive Mr. Dyson.

Peace had caught up with the Dysons again on the afternoon they moved house to a different part of Sheffield. He followed the furniture van and got to the house before them. When they arrived, they found him sitting in one of their own chairs, grinning evilly. "You see," he leered, "I'm here to annoy you, wherever you go. You'll never escape me."

The day after the Habron trial, Peace visited a pub in Sheffield and started drinking heavily. Urged on by the mob, he improvized a musical instrument from a tautened length of string and, using a stick as a bow, began playing with increasing frenzy. Within a few hours, he had worked himself into a paroxysm of hate. Suddenly throwing down his stick, he stumbled out of the pub in the

direction of the Dysons' new home.

At about 9 p.m. Mrs. Dyson left her kitchen and walked down the back garden to the outside lavatory. She was horrified to find Peace hiding inside. As he made a grab for her, she screamed. Her husband heard the cry and ran to her aid, knowing instinctively who was at the bottom of the dark garden. Peace was trapped. He fired once, but Mr. Dyson, as brave as the ill-fated P.C. Cock, bore down on him. Peace fired once more, and this time the bullet smashed into Mr. Dyson's left temple. He died nearly two hours later.

### Narrow escape

A nationwide manhunt was launched for Peace. Posters announcing "WANTED FOR MURDER—£100 REWARD" appeared all over Britain. Now Peace needed every one of his thousand faces.

By a combination of cunning, skill and sheer effrontery, he kept one step ahead of the police. He got out of his brother's house in Hull—where he had called to collect some clothes—only 30 minutes before the police arrived. He was actually having breakfast with his wife when the police swooped on her shop, but he managed to get away over the rooftops. He even found time to pick up a mistress, Sue Bailey.

He was in bed with her in lodgings in Nottingham when police broke into the room. It was part of a routine check on

119

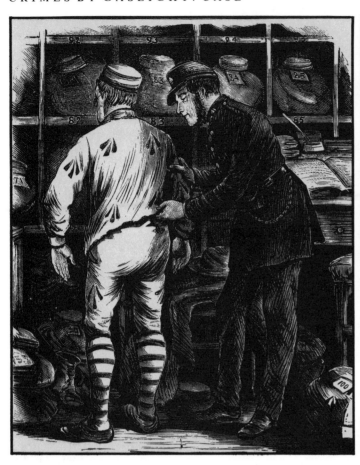

receivers of stolen property. Peace pretended to be a travelling salesman, and while Sue kept the policeman talking, he went downstairs under the pretext of fetching up his samples. Still in his socks, he squeezed through the narrow bars of a downstairs window and made off. Half an hour later, after the fuss had died down, he sent a neighbour back into the house to fetch his boots.

After that narrow escape, Peace felt he deserved a holiday. Posing as "Mr. and Mrs. Thompson", Peace and Sue Bailey stayed for two months in the home of a police-sergeant in Aubury Road, Hull. He was regarded as an ideal lodger, particularly as he seemed to show a genuine interest in the policeman's work.

As far as Peace was concerned, the house made an ideal "cover" for burgling expeditions. He cut a swathe through Hull, breaking into as many as seven houses in one night. In one house, he was surprised when the occupants returned early from a dinner. He stood on the stairs and fired a shot into the ceiling. As the occupants scattered for cover, he dived out of a window and escaped over the garden wall. He also fired at an unarmed policeman who stopped him as he left another house. Sensibly, the policeman let him go.

At the end of his "working holiday" Peace decided that Hull was becoming too dangerous, despite the unwitting

**UNFAMILIAR GUISE . . . Charles Peace was accustomed to changing his clothes — it helped him avoid recognition — but prison uniform had a different function!**

protection afforded by his policeman landlord. He packed his housebreaking tools in his violin-case and took a train to London.

On the way, he was joined by a taciturn middle-aged man who resisted all Peace's efforts to strike up a conversation. Gradually, however, Peace started to draw him out. He was startled to discover that the man was William Marwood, the official executioner. It was a bizarre confrontation. As Marwood left, Peace shook him by the hand and said, "If you ever have to do the job for me, be sure you grease the rope well to let me slip." Marwood looked at the decrepit old man with the white hair, whiskers and nut-brown face and laughed at such a remote possibility. Two years later the two men were to meet again, under rather more strained circumstances.

**Babbling outburst**

In London, Peace created a completely new image for himself, one which conformed to all the Victorian ideals of middle-class respectability. As "Mr. and Mrs. Thompson", he and Sue Bailey set up home at 5, East Terrace, Evelina Road, Peckham. They were joined by his

wife, Hannah, posing as a lodger.

It was a cosy existence. In the evenings, Peace would invite the neighbours in for musical entertainment. With Sue at the piano, he would play favourite airs on his violin, or sing one of the sentimental ballads of the period. The guests would be urged to join in a new hymn by the evangelists Ira Sankey and D. L. Moody, whose volume "Sacred Songs and Solos" was currently uplifting many a Victorian parlour. Maybe "Mr. Thompson" would be persuaded to give a moralizing recitation, possibly the one ending "And as we journey down life's road, Be good to one another"!

The evening would end early, for Mr. Thompson was known to disapprove of late nights. A final potter round the plants growing profusely in the parlour, a handful of food for his pet birds, a final check whether the pony was comfortable in its stable at the bottom of the garden, and the Thompsons would be in bed by 10.30. The Queen herself could not have disapproved of their restrained and exemplary way of life.

By some strange coincidence, the arrival of the Thompsons in Peckham coincided with an unprecedented wave of burglaries throughout London and southern England. Lord Shaftesbury's home was raided and half his belongings stolen. Six weeks later, the same burglar struck again and removed the remaining half.

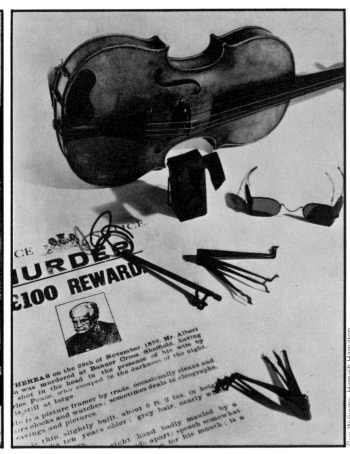

The police were swamped with complaints from irate householders. There was no limit to the man's audacity.

When the raider was thwarted by a particularly stubborn office safe, he calmly left the building, broke into the proprietor's house, lifted the key from the man's trouser-pocket while he slept and returned to finish the job. It was said that he carried away his loot in a cart drawn by a pony that had been trained to tread lightly and silently on the cobbles.

P.C. R202 Edward Robinson was therefore particularly alert as he patrolled his beat in Blackheath, in south London, early on the morning of October 10, 1878. Just after 2 a.m. he noticed a flicker of light in the window of a mansion. It was instantly extinguished, only to glimmer briefly again in another window. With P.C. R284 William Girling, P.C. Robinson circled the mansion. P.C. Girling whispered, "I'll ring the doorbell and you keep watch outside." At the first clamour of the bell, a window on the ground floor was flung open and a nimble figure headed for the back wall. P.C. Robinson hurled himself forward. The man turned, levelled a revolver and said, "Keep off, keep back, or by God I'll shoot you!"

For the third time, a courageous figure walked steadily towards the gun-barrel pointed by Charlie Peace. There were three shots, the final one missing P.C. Robinson's head by a hairsbreadth. The

**STOCK IN TRADE . . . With his violin and one or two special "tools", Charlie had all he needed to make a living . . . Right: His abortive attempt to escape.**

constable rushed at Peace, his momentum carrying him on despite a shot which tore into his arm. Peace collapsed under the weight of the constable, desperately wriggling to get away. But P.C. Robinson held on with one hand until P.C. Girling ran up and paralysed Peace's gun-arm with a blow from his truncheon. "Let me up," whined the prisoner. "I'll come quietly. I only did it to frighten him so I could get away."

On November 19, Charlie Peace – his identity revealed by the treacherous Sue Bailey – appeared at the Old Bailey, charged with the attempted murder of P.C. Robinson. The jury quickly returned their verdict of Guilty.

In a babbling outburst, Peace pleaded with the Judge for leniency. "Oh, my Lord, I know I am base and bad to the uttermost, but I know at the same time they have painted my case blacker than it really is. I hope you will take all this into consideration and not pass upon me a sentence of imprisonment that will be the means of my dying in prison, where it is possible that I shall not have the chance among my associates to prepare to meet my God that I hope I shall meet. "So, my Lord, do have mercy upon

me. I beseech you, give me a chance, my Lord, to regain my freedom, and you shall not, with the help of my God, have cause to repent passing a merciful sentence upon me. Oh, my Lord, you yourself expect mercy from the hands of your great and merciful God. Oh, my Lord, do have mercy upon me, a most wretched, miserable man that is not fit to die. I am not fit to live, but with the help of my God I will try to become a good man. I will try to become a man that will be able in the last day to meet my God, my Great Judge, to receive the great reward at His hands for my true repentance. Lord, have mercy on me!"

### Not bad enough!

Mr. Justice Hawkins, however, was not feeling in a merciful mood. He sent Peace to jail for life. The question of Peace's sentence was purely academic, for Peace now had to face trial for the murder of Mr. Dyson. The police had brought Mrs. Dyson back from America, where she had emigrated, to identify Peace. Mrs. Dyson wasn't in a merciful vein, either. "The place to which the wicked go is not bad enough for him," she said. "No matter where he goes, I am satisfied there will be a Hell."

Each day during the trial, Peace had to be taken by train from Pentonville Prison to Sheffield Assizes. On the third day, he tried to make a break for it. Without warning, he somersaulted out of the window while the train was travelling at 50 m.p.h. Dangling outside the carriage, Peace tried to kick himself free from P.C. Robertson, who was clinging to his ankle. Finally, Peace's boot worked free and he fell in a heap at the side of the track as the train rushed past.

When the train arrived at Sheffield with an empty compartment where Peace should have been, the word went round that he had escaped. Huge crowds outside the Town Hall had to be reassured by the Chief Constable that the murderer had been recaptured.

### Macabre laugh

Wrapped in blankets and presenting a pitiful sight, Peace tried to play on the sympathy of the jury. "I'm a sick man," he whined. "I shouldn't be here. It's not justice." The jury took 10 minutes to find him Guilty. The Judge sentenced him to death.

Realizing that no amount of cunning or humbug could save him from the gallows, Peace asked to see the Rev. J. H. Littlewood, his vicar back at Darnell. He

Sheffield Newspapers

**THE CONDEMNED CONVICT (left and below). By the date of his execution he was a forlorn and broken figure—though he still enjoyed the hangman's surprise.**

dictated a complete confession of his crimes, including the murder of P.C. Cock, for which young William Habron was still breaking boulders at Portland Jail. "You'll find that the bullet which killed the policeman was fired from my revolver," he said. "And if you remove a bullet from a live cartridge, you will see the murder bullet fits it exactly." The bullet *did* fit, and Habron was released with a gift of £800.

"There's one other thing that has been on my mind for years," he told the vicar. Mr. Littlewood braced himself for another dreadful revelation. With injured innocence, Peace explained, "I never did steal your Sunday School clock. Your accusation had caused me much grief and pain. I would rather have given you a clock, and much more besides, than have stolen it."

On February 25, 1879, aged 47, Charles Peace went to the scaffold at Armley Jail, Leeds, after urging his relatives to lead God-fearing lives. "What is the scaffold?" he asked just before he left the condemned cell. "Just a short cut to Heaven." But Peace had one final, macabre laugh before the trap swung open. It was the astonished look on the face of the hangman, William Marwood, confronted again with the little old man in the railway carriage.

Mary Evans

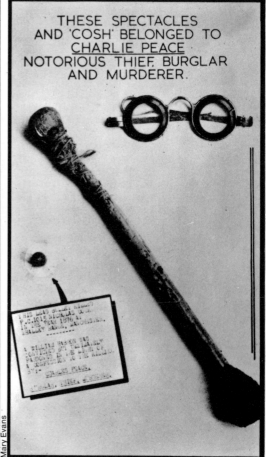

THESE SPECTACLES AND 'COSH' BELONGED TO CHARLIE PEACE NOTORIOUS THIEF, BURGLAR AND MURDERER.

Slim Hewitt

Radio Times Hulton, Mary Evans

# MADDENED BY GREED

James Blomfield Rush can only be described as a nasty, venomous man. His life was governed by two passions: blinding hatred of those who stood in his way and an unbridled lust for money. He satisfied both with murder . . .

THE house looked like a battlefield. In the porch, Mr. Isaac Jermy lay spread-eagled, his heart blown to pieces by gun-shot. Inside the house, his son, Mr. Jermy Jermy, lay dead with a hole in his chest. Near him, screaming with pain, staggered Mr. Jermy Jermy's wife, Sophia, her arm almost blown off. A few yards farther on, maidservant Eliza Chestney slumped against a wall, her hip riddled with lead shot.

An invading army could not have left behind a more appalling scene of massacre than the one which greeted police when they arrived at Stanfield Hall, in the lonely, brooding fenland of Norfolk; yet they knew exactly where to go and whom to

arrest. By dawn, they had surrounded Potash Farm, the isolated home of James Blomfield Rush, a mile away across muddy fields from Stanfield Hall.

Rush offered no resistance; indeed, his whole attitude reflected injured inno-cence rather than guilt. Told that he was being arrested for attempting to wipe out the entire Jermy family, his reply was a classic of understatement. "Good God, I hope they don't think it is me; 'tis a rather serious offence."

But Rush's puzzled air didn't fool the police. Everyone in Norfolk knew that people had a nasty habit of dying when Rush was around. Years earlier, his wife had died in mysterious circumstances

after bearing him nine children. He promptly took a mistress, a music-teacher named Emily Sandford, and they lived together at Potash Farm.

Not long afterwards, Rush's stepfather was killed in an odd shooting incident in his own kitchen. He had been admiring his shotgun — an expensive and superior weapon — when it suddenly went off, blowing his head apart. The only other person in the house had been James Blomfield Rush, who had dropped in for a chat after a day's hunting. At the in-quest, the jury reluctantly returned a ver-dict of "Accidental death".

James Blomfield Rush hadn't finished pruning the family tree. For his mother,

Mary Evans

Mary Rush, was unlucky enough to inherit all his stepfather's cash and property. Nobody was surprised when Mary Rush suddenly fell ill. On a Sunday night, James Blomfield Rush was left alone with his ailing mother. Her nurse returned to find him feeding her with cake moistened with "what looked like wine". A few hours later, Mrs. Mary Rush was dead. She left everything to James Blomfield Rush's nine children; a mistake which Rush corrected by forging a codicil to her will, making over all the inheritance to himself, until his youngest child reached the age of 21.

With his family neatly disposed of, Rush was free to devote his attention to the Jermys. For years—ever since Isaac Jermy had taken over Stanfield Hall—Rush had pursued them with a vendetta of almost Sicilian ferocity. There were a dozen reasons for the feud—all of them stemming from Rush's paranoid hatred of Isaac Jermy, the owner of Stanfield Hall and chief legal officer for Norwich.

### Genocide

For a start, Rush believed Isaac Jermy was not entitled to the Hall. Before Isaac Jermy appeared on the scene, Rush had leased two farms, including the Stanfield Hall farm, from Jermy's father. When the old man died, there was a furious dispute over the ownership of the Hall, and Rush had sided with two other members of the family, Thomas Jermy and John Larner.

The row reached such a pitch that Larner—the more belligerent of the two claimants—led a raid on the Hall and tried to occupy it by force. Isaac Jermy

**ELEGANT and stately, Stanfield Hall was an unlikely setting for a savage, mass murder. The map (right) shows its position in relation to Potash Farm.**

wasn't standing for that. Using his authority as Recorder of Norwich, he called in the army, and while Jermy stood on the lawn reading the Riot Act, soldiers of the 4th Dragoon Guards loaded their muskets and pointed them at the raiders, who were perched on the roof and standing at the windows. The riot fizzled out within minutes.

All this did not endear Rush to his new landlord, who lost no time getting his own back. Gleefully, Isaac Jermy discovered that Rush's leasehold documents had not been properly drawn up, and he used this as an excuse to increase the rents. By then, Rush already had his eye on a third farm owned by Jermy. Despite the serious drain on his resources, he bought it—although he had to borrow the cash from Jermy.

Rush ended up owing Jermy a total of £5000, with a 4 per cent interest adding another £200 each year. Under the terms of the agreement, the whole sum had to be payed back by November 30, 1848, an obligation which placed Rush irredeemably in debt. Though, theoretically, Potash Farm was a money-maker, standing on rich and productive land, Rush had one drawback. He was a rotten farmer, and under his poor husbandry Potash Farm failed to achieve its potential. Seeing his repayments threatened, Isaac Jermy used his position as landlord to bring an action for miscultivation of the farm—so increasing Rush's hatred.

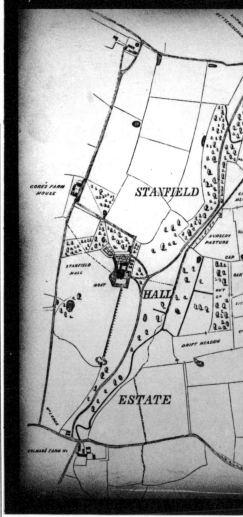

Hatred came easily to James Blomfield Rush; his fellow villagers regarded him with a mixture of fear and contempt, not least because he was a brutish, thickset man whose violent and deceitful nature brought him into constant conflict with the law. At various times he had been accused of seduction, arson and incitement to riot.

But there was a weapon anyone could use against him. He was illegitimate, a

**ISOLATED and, in Rush's hands, a money loser, it was here at Potash Farm that the killer planned his desperate attack on the unlucky Jermy household.**

mortgage debt on Potash Farm. Even the annual interest was beyond him.

It was at this point that James Blomfield Rush hit on the solution. Genocide had worked well before in getting him his father's misdirected inheritance; there was no reason why it shouldn't succeed in ridding him of his tormentors at Stanfield Hall: he would annihilate the whole Jermy tribe.

With devious cunning, Rush began to play both ends against the middle, for whether the Jermys ended up dead or alive, he would be clear of his debt. The first move was to make use of the "Stanfield Hall claimants", Thomas Jermy and John Larner. Their claim for ownership was still simmering, slightly hampered by the fact that neither could read or write. Rush was the answer to their prayers. Feigning enthusiasm for their campaign, he persuaded them to sign an agreement wiping out the debt and substituting a nominal rent in the event of their gaining Stanfield Hall, in turn for his support.

The two men were too stupid to see that the document could have a more sinister interpretation. In a court of law, their "X's" at the bottom of the agreement implied a conspiracy to oust Isaac Jermy from Stanfield Hall. With the incriminating document safely in his pocket, Rush started on the second stage of his plan. This was a simple matter of forgery, no more difficult than the phoney codicil to his mother's will.

Using Emily Sandford as a reluctant witness, Rush manufactured three agreements, purporting to have been signed by Isaac Jermy, cancelling the debt on Potash Farm and reducing the rents on the other two properties. As his part of the bargain, Rush promised to surrender a sheaf of wholly fictitious "papers and documents" which cast doubt on Jermy's right to Stanfield Hall.

### Shattered figure

It was now November 27, 1848. In three days' time the debt on Potash Farm fell due, and Rush's forged agreements would be worthless. Isaac Jermy's hand had to be halted within 72 hours, or the only roof over Rush's head would be the one on Norwich debtors' jail. He had to move fast. On the afternoon of the 27th he ordered a labourer to lay down some straw on the footpath which ran from Potash Farm to the lawn of Stanfield Hall. The path had never been covered that far before, but the labourer shrugged his shoulders and asked no questions.

There was still one vital document to fabricate. The following morning, Rush tore a page from a notebook and penned a strange message. "There are seven of us here," it said, "three of us outside and four inside the hall, all armed as you see us two. If any of your servants offer to leave the premises or to follow, you will be shot dead. Therefore, all of you keep in the servants' hall and you nor anyone else will take any harm, for we are only come to take. of the Stanfield Hall property."

The note was signed "Thomas Jermy" and was clearly intended to implicate him

humiliating fact which made him socially inferior to even the most vacant-eyed yokel. Rush felt the stigma bitterly. The whole world, he believed, was united in a conspiracy to thwart his efforts and deny his rights.

With the millstone of Potash Farm round his neck, Rush drifted deeper into debt. In May 1847 he was declared bankrupt, which meant he could neither cash cheques nor hope to pay the coming

in the bloodbath at Stanfield Hall. But in his haste, Rush made one disastrous mistake: he forgot that the real Thomas Jermy couldn't write his own name.

That evening, Rush had planned to take Emily Sandford to a concert. But, on the pretext of feeling unwell, he cried off. At 7.30 p.m., while Emily was reading a book, he left the parlour and went to his room. He put on a false wig and a long cloak with a hood that partly covered his face. Slipping the warning note into his pocket, he picked up a double-barrelled blunderbuss that had been converted for quick-loading and set off across the fields to massacre the Jermys, his boots leaving no footprints on the carefully prepared straw.

At the entrance to the Hall he dropped the note where he knew it would be spotted. Then, pulling his hood over his face, he walked in to begin the carnage.

On Thursday, March 29, 1849 – the first day of the trial of James Blomfield Rush at Norwich Assizes – a path was cleared through the spectators in the courtroom. Two men entered, bearing a covered stretcher, rather like a half-open coffin. In it was the shattered figure of Eliza Chestney, one of the only two people who survived the murderous blasts from Rush's blunderbuss. Her wounds

**CRIPPLED by wounds, Eliza Chestney was carried to court in a specially made litter. Once there, her graphic account of Rush's attack horrified the jury . . .**

had not healed and she was still in pain, but she could recall every moment of that night of terror.

"It was about eight at night," she told the court. "I heard a gun, then another and then a groan. When I got to the staircase hall, I saw Mr. Jermy Jermy lying on the floor. I then saw a man coming from the dining-room door, and he had what appeared to me to be a shot gun up to his shoulder. I levelled it and shot me. I did not fall directly. Another shot followed at once, and I saw my mistress's arm twirl about. I twisted round several times and fell down. I gave three violent shrieks and said I was going to die and no one would come and help me. I remember no more until I awoke at the bottom of the staircase."

Prosecuting Counsel: Did you recognize the man who shot you and your mistress?

Chestney: Yes. The prisoner. I have seen him several times at Stanfield Hall. I saw both the head of the man and his shoulders. Mr. Rush has a way of carrying his head which can't be mistaken. No

person ever came to Stanfield with such an appearance beside himself.

Another servant, who escaped the hail of gunshot, was equally sure that Rush was the gunman. Martha Reed described how she heard shots, followed by screams. "Miss Jermy came running into the servants' hall. She said, 'Oh, Read, we shall all be murdered!' I then saw a man coming along the passage, about seven yards from Miss Jermy. He had some firearm in his right hand, larger than a usual-sized pistol. He was a low, stout man. I have repeatedly seen Rush in the Hall. The man was of the height, size and carriage of Rush, and as soon as I saw him my impression was that it was Rush, and that is my impression still."

**Damning evidence**

In the dock, the "low, stout man" glowered at the witnesses. Disdaining counsel, Rush had elected to conduct his own defence. His tactics consisted of abuse, threats, cajolery, furious protestations of innocence, constant interruptions and appeals to the Almighty. His menacing attitude left many witnesses shaken. "Recollect you are on your oath," he warned one witness, before beginning his cross-examination. "This trial is one of life and death to me. My firm hope is in

God, and as His eye is on you, as you wish to walk out of this Court in health, speak the truth."

The judge, Baron Rolfe, leaned over backwards to give him a fair hearing. But the more latitude Rush received, the more truculent he became. Gradually, the court sensed that his anger was building up to his confrontation with Emily Sandford, his former mistress and now the crucial prosecution witness. They were right. As soon as her name was called, Rush turned with fury on the judge.

Rush: I have a higher power than you, My Lord, and I say to this witness that I am innocent of this charge.

Judge: It will be for the jury to say so.

Rush: But *I* must say so, and caution her to speak the truth.

Judge: If she does not speak the truth, she will be subject to the penalty of perjury in this life and punishment in the next.

Rush: I have never had an opportunity of speaking to her, but I wish to tell her to consider what sort of evidence she is about to give.

Judge: You will do yourself no good by . . .

Rush: I cannot help it! I can prove my innocence! I have never been angry with her from the start . . . although she

**PHYSICALLY SHATTERED but mentally very much alive, Eliza Chestney evoked the sympathy of all who heard her. She stood up well to Rush's cross-examination.**

contradicted the evidence she gave at the first hearing.

Judge: I cannot allow this. You are entitled to be in court while the evidence is given, but if you misconduct yourself you will be removed.

Emily Sandford was pale and thin, she had just given birth to Rush's illegitimate child, but her evidence, given coolly and clearly, was damning. She remembered him leaving the house at around 7.30 on the evening of the shooting. As he passed the parlour, he called out, "Fasten the door after me." Around 9.30 she heard him knocking at the door. He said "It's only me, open up", and she undid the bolt and returned to the room. He went straight upstairs, but came down to the parlour a few minutes later. He looked pale, ill and agitated.

"I asked him what was the matter and if anything had happened. He replied, 'No, nothing; if you hear any enquiries for me, say I was out only ten minutes.' Later, I went into his room and asked him where I should sleep. He told me to sleep in my own room, although I always

used to sleep in the same bed as him. I noticed that he had a fire burning brightly, although I hadn't lit it."

Emily didn't realize it then, but the fire had already swallowed up the muddy boots in which Rush had trudged to Stanfield Hall. Around 2.30 in the morning, Emily was woken by Rush knocking at her bedroom door. He came to her bed and told her, "You must be firm. If anybody asks you how long I was out, say ten minutes."

**Unadulterated venom**

As soon as Emily Sandford finished giving evidence, Rush jumped to his feet to cross-examine. Emily's ordeal had only just started. It was to last for another 12 hours. At first, Rush began quietly, playing on Emily's old affection for him. He suggested that Emily could have confused the time he left and returned, as her watch had been three-quarters of an hour fast. When Emily stuck to her original statement, Rush raised the possibility that she was so immersed in her book that she lost all track of the time.

Rush: Now, I want you to recollect yourself. You say you began to read after I left on the evening of the 28th?

Emily: Yes.

Rush: Was I away, do you think, more

127

than half an hour?

Emily: Yes, I should think you were away until nine o'clock.

Rush: Now I ask you on oath, given on a solemn occasion like the present, if you think I was absent more than half an hour?

Emily: It is impossible to say exactly, as I was reading an amusing work. You appeared to return sooner than I expected.

Rush: If you can recollect the name of the work, perhaps it will assist you in giving a correct answer?

Emily: The name was *Whitefriars, or the Days of Charles II*.

Rush: Now, I ask you from what you were reading, do you think I was absent more than half an hour?

Emily: Yes, I should say a great deal more. I read half the volume while you were away.

### Broken promise

Cajolery having failed to get the answers he wanted, Rush adopted a more intimidating tone. "I must caution you how to answer," he snapped, "unless you wish to swear my life away falsely. If you wish to do so, say so at once, and I will not ask you another question."

There was a cry of "Shame!" from the courtroom, and even the indulgently patient judge warned Rush that he would not tolerate any browbeating of witnesses, but Rush had got the bit between his teeth. After a few deferential questions, he returned to the attack, accusing Emily of betraying him out of spite.

Rush: Have you not told me that I should repent the day that I did not make you my wife?

Emily: I told you you would never prosper after the day you refused to make me your wife, or something like it. But that was two years ago. I told you you would not prosper after you had broken your promise, and you have not.

Rush: Have you ever told me that I should not marry anybody else but you?

Emily: You have told me so. You told me so when I charged you with being unfaithful. You said repeatedly that I had made you a reformed man.

Again there was an interruption from the courtroom. "Poor, pitiful thing!" shouted a woman. Rush gave her a look of unadulterated venom. He had tried to shake Emily's evidence, and failed. The irony of the situation must have occurred to Rush. If he had "made an honest woman" of Emily, as he had promised, she could not have given evidence against him. No wife can be forced to testify against her husband. But a mistress can.

Little wonder that Rush had turned on Emily when she had first signed the damaging evidence against him before the trial. George Pinson, governor of Norwich Jail, recalled Rush's outburst. "I heard the prisoner say, 'If you sign that,' pointing to the statements, 'I hope your hand will rot.'"

But Rush had already signed his own life away. A handwriting expert testified that the various papers and agreements apparently signed by Thomas Jermy and Isaac Jermy were, in fact, in Rush's handwriting, and so was the warning note dropped in Stanfield Hall.

In the dock, Rush glowered. Maybe he had just realized his stupid mistake in signing the illiterate Thomas Jermy's name to the note. If he hadn't, the next witness clinched it, for it was Thomas Jermy. His evidence consisted of two words. But they must have shattered Rush's overweening confidence.

Counsel: Can you write?

Thomas Jermy: No, sir.

Counsel: That is all I have to ask him.

For once, Rush was speechless. "No questions," he growled.

### Astonishing harangue

Late on the fourth day the prosecution closed its case, and the stage was set for Rush to appear as his own defence counsel. But he was in no hurry. "I trust, My Lord," he asked the judge, "that you will not call on me at this late hour to commence my defence?" "Do you not think yourself able to do justice to it?" said the judge innocently. "No, My Lord," Rush replied, "not at this late hour of the day." It was the barest hint of what James Rush had in store.

In his cell that night, Rush was even more demanding than usual. The prison staff had become resigned to his tantrums, particularly his unctuous piety. "Thank God I am quite comfortable in body and mind," he told the governor. "I eat well, drink well, and sleep well." Even the prison chaplains had tired of his arrogant self-righteousness and his constant appeals for "God to witness my innocence".

They were lucky. They were not at Norwich Assizes the following morning, Tuesday, April 3, 1849, to hear the most extraordinary defence ever presented by a prisoner in a British court. Before a dazed judge and jury and a courtroom stunned by disbelief, Rush spoke for 14 hours non-stop. It was an astonishing harangue, wild, illogical and demented; a rambling tirade of self-justification and wounded innocence, punctuated by fierce appeals to the Almighty.

Rush flailed at every target in sight. The only respite came when he started babbling about a "foreign body", referred to by one of the prosecution's medical witnesses. He clearly had no idea of the meaning of the phrase, and the judge intervened.

"You do not understand it," said Baron Rolfe mildly. "Medical gentlemen, when they find anything in the flesh which is of a different nature, call it a foreign body . . ." It made little difference. The judge's explanation was swept aside in a torrent of words.

At last, with judge, jury and officials

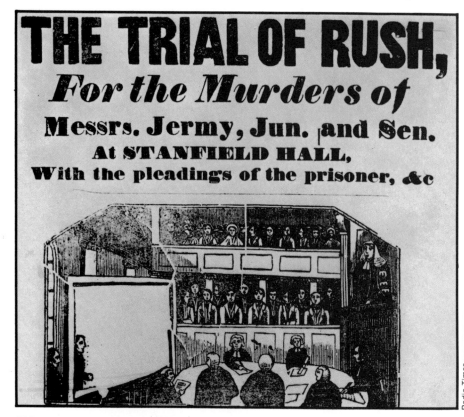

THE TRIAL OF RUSH,
*For the Murders of*
Messrs. Jermy, Jun. and Sen.
AT STANFIELD HALL,
With the pleadings of the prisoner, &c

Mary Evans

"The others, if there are any against me, will bless you in their dying moments that you did not allow them to return a verdict of 'guilty' against an innocent man. I have not the slightest doubt that at one time or other it will come out who were the real perpetrators of this most horrid deed. I say again, gentlemen, trust to God and do your duty; do not be led away from the facts of the case by the flowery eloquence that may be used against me by the learned gentlemen employed against me.

"All I can say is, may God Almighty bless you and make you discern with a wise and understanding heart. This is the prayer of one who expects justice at your hands for the sake of his dear little children, who are destitute of a mother and who are looking to you to give them back their father."

The marathon was over. In his closing speech, Serjeant John Barnard Byles, Chief Prosecuting Counsel, could not resist the observation that "the present trial has exceeded in the annals of judicial long-suffering anything that has ever been experienced". One look at the judge, sitting exhausted on the Bench, was sufficient confirmation.

### Malevolent spirit

After Rush's 14 hours of ranting demagogery, the speed of the jury's decision took the court by surprise. After a mere 10 minutes they returned a verdict of guilty. Rush looked as though he would have liked to strangle each juryman personally. "My Lord," he barked, "I an innocent of that, thank God Almighty."

As he placed the black cap upon his head, the judge was no longer the patient, tolerant figure anxious to extend every concession to the prisoner in the dock.

**MOST DAMNING** of all the witnesses was Rush's mistress, Emily Sandford (above). Outside the court at Norwich hundreds gathered to hear the verdict . . .

visibly wilting, Rush reached his peroration. His eyes bulged, and he was panting and bathed in sweat. His burly, aggressive figure seemed to burst out of the dock as he invoked the Almighty to rescue the jury from the most disastrous mistake of their lives.

"I am sure that God in His goodness will influence your verdict in my favour. My whole trust is in Him and that He may guide you. Should there be — which I cannot see how there should be — a division as to your opinion, be ruled by me and trust in God — those who are for me — and you will afterwards think it the happiest day of your lives, when you stood firm, and on no account whatever would return any other verdict than that of 'not guilty'.

EXTERIOR OF THE COURT AT NORWICH.

Radio Times

"There is no one who has witnessed your conduct during the trial and heard the evidence disclosed against you," he said, "that will not feel with me when I tell you that you must quit this world by an ignominious death, an object of unmitigated abhorrence to everyone." He then sentenced Rush to death.

The morning of April 21, 1849, was dull and drizzly. The wind whipped the rain against the walls of Norwich Castle and along the small bridge on which the gallows had been set. But by midday the sky had cleared, and with the sun came the crowds. They came by coach and train, by pony-and-trap and horseback, on foot or on their parents' shoulders, until more than 13,000 people covered the entire area around the scaffold, many perched on the rooftops and the church tower.

Inside the Castle, James Blomfield Rush was far from subdued. Pressed by the prison chaplains for a last-minute confession, Rush turned on them so

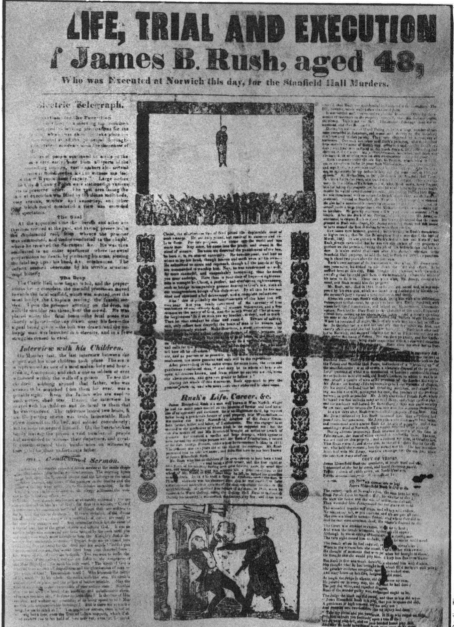

RUSH.

**HEADLINE NEWS . . . The national press seized on the murder details with relish (above). There were some amusing aspects to the case, like Rush's disguise (top left). Below left: His death mask . . .**

violently he had to be restrained. He was still protesting when John Calcroft, the executioner, pinioned his arms. Rush marched resolutely to the scaffold, shaking his head as if to say, "What a scandal that an innocent man should hang."

On the platform, he turned his back to the crowd and issued a few brisk orders to the hangman. "This doesn't go easy," he said, as Calcroft adjusted the noose. "Put the thing a little higher. Take your time. Don't be in a hurry."

They were his last words. The trapdoor shot open, and he was swallowed into the platform. He was 49. The crowd made

no sound as he went.

Wife, mother, father, the Jermys, both father and son, Mrs. Jermy and her crippled maidservant . . . James Blomfield Rush cut a swathe of tragedy wherever he went. His baleful influence now followed the only survivor to the ends of the earth. A generous local squire, Sir John Boileau, sent Emily Sandford to start a new life in Australia.

He paid her bills, gave her a letter of introduction to the Bishop of Melbourne and bought her a piano so she could continue teaching. But her notoriety had sped ahead of her. When her identity was discovered, she was harassed, mobbed and persecuted. There was no work for her. Emily Sandford became Rush's final victim, his malevolent spirit reaching out to her from beyond the grave. And one morning she killed herself.

# THE A-Z OF CRIME

THE clerk in the diamond dealer's office in London's Hatton Garden took delivery of the registered parcel at midday on July 16, 1913. Hurriedly he carried it in to his employer, Max Mayer, a well-known dealer in precious stones. "It's the necklace from Paris, sir," he exclaimed. "It's arrived!" Mayer looked eagerly on as the clerk broke the seal, cut the string, and lifted out a small cardboard box. The clerk opened the box and held it up for Mayer to see. Abruptly the smile died on the dealer's face. For instead of the 61-pearl necklace he was expecting there were some lumps of sugar!

The necklace—worth some £150,000 and consisting of oriental graduated pearls—was one of the finest in the world. It had taken Mayer years to "build it up", and early in 1913 he had sent it to his Paris agent, Henri Salamons, whose premises were just behind the Opera. He had heard from Salamons that a wealthy Frenchman was interested in buying the necklace. Negotiations went

## T

## THEFT

on slowly throughout the spring, neither party could come to terms, and eventually the deal fell through.

At 4 p.m. on July 15 Salamons went to the post office in the Rue de Provence and sent the necklace back to Mayer. The next thing he heard was a telegram from London stating: BOX ARRIVED BUT NO NECKLACE. It was clear that the pearls had been stolen somewhere between Paris and Hatton Garden, and leading detectives of the Sûreté and Scotland Yard were called in.

In London, Chief Inspector Ward (who the previous year had been in charge of the notorious Seddon poisoning case) posted a reward of £10,000 for "information leading to the apprehension of the thief or thieves, and the recovery of the property". In Paris, M. Puichard, head

**ONE OF THE FINEST necklaces in the world, 61 pearls worth £150,000, took years to build up. But somewhere between Paris and London it vanished.**

MR MAYER'S OFFICE — IN HATTON GARDEN

MR MAX MAYER.

MR SALAMONS.

THE OBLONG REPRESENTS A POSTAGE STAMP DRAWN ON THE SAME SCALE AS THE NECKLACE TO SHOW SIZE OF PEARLS

THE CIRCLE REPRESENTS A 6D PIECE DRAWN ON THE SAME SCALE AS THE NECKLACE TO SHOW SIZE OF PEARLS.

THE STOLEN NECKLACE.

of the French C.I.D., interviewed a waiter who worked near to the post office, and learnt of a "suspicious-looking man" who had ordered coffee at the café on the day of the robbery and then pocketed six lumps of sugar.

Nothing more definite emerged until August, when Samuel Brandstater, an Antwerp jewel merchant, was approached by Leisir Gutwirth, a diamond broker from north London. Gutwirth stated that he was "in possession" of the missing necklace and was prepared to part with it for half a million francs. A few days later, after thinking the proposition over, Brandstater travelled to London, saw Inspector Ward, and agreed to meet Gutwirth for a second time and to "play him like a fish".

An appointment was made for the two men to meet at Charing Cross station, and from there they went to the Golden Cross Hotel for drinks. Gutwirth announced that the "selling price" had gone up to a million French francs, and suggested a further meeting "to discuss the

**THE GANG was large and well organized. It included (clockwise from top left) James Lockett, Simon Silverman, Joseph Grizzard and Leisir Gutwirth.**

matter" the following day. This time the men met each other in a Lyons teashop, and this time they were kept under observation by plainclothes detectives. They were joined by two more "diamond merchants", Joseph Grizzard, who was already known to the police as a crook and a conman, and another noted criminal, James Lockett.

After sipping tea in the shop in Kingsway, off the Strand, Grizzard took out a cigarette and asked Lockett for a light. His companion produced a box of matches, threw it onto the table, and Grizzard carefully opened it. Inside, in place of the matchsticks, were three lustrous pearls lying on a bed of cotton-wool. "There are more where they came from," said Lockett airily. "Just find me a buyer."

When this was reported to Inspector Ward he realized that he was dealing with a large and well-organized gang. This was demonstrated at the next meeting, when one Simon Silverman (an Austrian, like Grizzard) sat across a table in the First Avenue Hotel from a reputable Paris pearl merchant, Max B. Spanier. At the request of the police, Spanier had agreed to act as a potential buyer, and was armed not only with thousands of francs but also with a gun.

After some preliminary discussion—when it was agreed that the pearls would be produced as a "show of goodwill"—the men parted and arranged to have further talks on the following Monday. For privacy they went to the hotel's billiard room, where Grizzard and Brandstater were already waiting. Spanier was handed a matchbox containing three pearls on a string, and a tin box with 58 top quality pearls in it. He immediately bought two of them for 100,000 francs, but this did not satisfy Grizzard.

"I cannot do business in dribs and drabs," he complained. "You must come to me with enough money on you to buy the lot. I am tired of these meetings. If we can't do business soon then the whole thing is off."

There followed one more meeting at the hotel, another stalemate situation, and a final appointment was made. The gang—Lockett, Grizzard, Silverman and Gutwirth—were to pick up Spanier outside the British Museum tube station. At the appointed time the crooks were there—and so were Inspector Ward and his assistants. The arrests were made quietly and without disturbance, and the Great Pearl Robbers duly stood trial at the Old Bailey.

There the prosecutor, Mr. Muir, stated that the coup had been planned by Silverman at a Hatton Garden restaurant known as the "Diamond Club". The conspirators then moved to Paris, where "Silverman, with a forged seal in his possession, was prepared to see the postman himself every morning. At one of these visits it was possible for the package to have been delivered to him, its seals altered, its contents taken out and other things substituted, and the parcel given back to the postman for delivery to Mr. Mayer."

Found guilty as charged, the four men received sentences of up to seven years in prison. All but three of the pearls were recovered when a needy piano-maker named Horne came across a matchbox lying in a north London street. He stooped, picked it up, and saw it contained what he thought were "white beads". He handed them in to the police, and kept one "bead" for himself—which he tried to sell "for a penny or a pint" in a pub, and then lost as he and his friends got drunk together.

# THIRD DEGREE

**PSYCHIATRICALLY UNFIT was the verdict on Detective-Sergeant Challenor. But how many rogue cops are there in any police force, and how are they discovered?**

BY 1931 the interrogative methods of the United States police were the scandal of the nation. In particular, people—both criminals and law-abiding citizens—were protesting about the use of the third degree. It was named, mockingly, after the third degree in freemasonry—a solemn and dignified ritual. And it came to mean what one American dictionary described as "use of brutal measures by the police in extorting information or a confession". The measures included the beating up of suspects with rubber hoses —the marks from which soon disappeared; the slapping about, or lifting up by their hair, of women; and the vicious and obscene torturing of Negroes.

Outcry by private citizens and members of the Press was noted by the National Commission on Law Observance and Enforcement, and in 1931 its officials made and completed their investigations, and published their Report. The Report found that the accusations against the police were appallingly true, and stated:

"To obtain confessions or admissions the officers (usually detectives) proceed 'to work' on the prisoner . . . If the prisoner refuses to answer, he may be returned to his cell with notice that he will stay till ready to 'come clean'. The cell may be specially chosen for the purpose—cold, dark, without bed or chair. The sweatbox is a small cell, completely dark and arranged to be heated till the prisoner, unable to bear the temperature, will promise to answer as described . . .

"Powerful lights turned full on the prisoner's face, or switched on and off, have been found effective. The electric chair is another device to extort confessions. The most commonly used method is persistent questioning, continuing hour after hour, sometimes by relays of officers. It has been known since 1500 at least that deprivation of sleep is the most effective torture and certain to produce any confession desired."

The Report found that some half of "these practices" were employed against defendants or suspects without criminal records. It established that crowds of people were sometimes apprehended in dragnet arrests, "without any definite evidence of their connection with any particular crime". It discovered that such methods were standard procedure in big cities such as New York, San Francisco, Chicago, and that the men so rounded up were kept standing under blinding lights, deprived of food or sleep, until they were completely exhausted and their powers of resistance gone.

"Some confessions," it stated, "have even been obtained by the police at the point of a gun. The law requires prompt production of a prisoner before a magistrate. In the large majority of cities where we have investigated, this rule has been and is being constantly violated."

The Report brought about a long-overdue improvement in the way police-men—arresting officers and station detec-tives—treated suspects. But it was too late to bring consolation to such out-and-out thugs as Peter Heslin, who held up a group of men on the corner of First Avenue and East 105th Street, New York, in the spring of 1926. Discovered in the act by Patrolman Charles Reilly, shots were fired, in which Heslin received a

bullet in the leg, and Reilly was mortally wounded. Following a trail of blood, policemen found the hoodlum hiding in a friend's apartment, and took him by stretcher and patrol wagon to the East 104th Street station.

There Heslin was dumped on a table in a back room wearing just his underwear. A detective took "pity" on him and threw a blood-soaked canvas over his shivering body. "We covered Charley Reilly with this," he snapped. "But he won't be needing it no more." Then, for the next several hours, the officers relentlessly tortured Heslin. They pounded his injured leg with a leather thong, and rubbed cigarette ash and dirt into the open wound. They ground out lighted cigarettes and cigars on his genitals. When he asked for something to drink they threw bowls of freezing water in his face.

Heslin survived to be electrocuted in July the following year. But despite what had happened to him—and the effects of the 1931 Report—the third degree had not completely been destroyed. Its use was not restricted to the United States only, for in 1963 it raised its vicious and

illegal head in England. It was the time of the Greek royal family's state visit to London. A number of political demonstrations were arranged, and one of the people involved in these was a young man named Donald Rooum. He was arrested while carrying a rolled-up banner, and was taken to West End Central police station.

He was quickly pounced upon by Detective-Sergeant H. G. Challenor—a 40-year-old rogue cop, feared by criminals and his colleagues alike. Twice Challenor smashed Rooum to the floor. He accused the prisoner of being ready to insult the Queen and her guests, and showed him a half-brick which he said Rooum had been intending to throw at the sovereigns. "Carrying an offensive weapon, me old darling," he chortled. "You can get two years for that!"

On reaching court, Rooum was awarded compensation when it was stated by an expert that no brick dust had been found in his pockets. He had not, as Challenor had asserted, been concealing a brick in his coat.

As a result of the case, Challenor—

who later retired from the force on pension—was found to be psychiatrically unfit to stand trial for "conspiring to pervert the course of justice". Some writers on the affair pointed out that the third degree had been used to extract confessions from both Jesus Christ and Joan of Arc, and that the evil was likely to always be with us.

But *The Times,* taking a more immediate and constructive view, asked: "Was it possible for a detective sergeant to remain on duty . . . after the onset of an acute form of paranoid schizophrenia . . . without someone or something being seriously at fault? . . . unless there existed . . . the atmosphere in which the lower ranks of a disciplined force know that . . . certain things . . . are contrary to regulations . . . and that they . . . are allowed to do those things provided they are not found out, and they know no one is going to try very hard to find out?"

**VICTIM Donald Rooum (ringed) with friends . . . Challenor's treatment of him proves just how easy it is for police to ignore the discipline of their work . . .**

THE edict to wipe out heretics—Moors and Hebrews—"by the way of fire" was issued by Pope Sixtus IV in November 1478. It gave King Ferdinand and Queen Isabella of Spain—who had divided the country between them—the right to arrest, imprison, and torture anyone who "defies or does not subscribe to the Roman Catholic faith". But such power, in itself, was not enough. They needed someone to implement it for them—someone cold, ruthless, without the "weakness" of pity. Someone like the Dominican friar, Tomás de Torquemada,

# TORQUEMADA

Isabella's confessor, and a fanatical enemy of the Jews and Mohammedans who secretly practised their religions in Spain.

Tall, gaunt, and stoop-shouldered, the 58-year-old friar lived the life that he preached. He never ate meat, he refused to wear linen, he slept on a bare plank, and his vow of poverty extended to his

sister—who became a nun as he would not provide for her. A stern figure in his order's black and white cloak, he already had great influence over Isabella, and he willingly accepted the post of inquisitor for Seville.

The inquisition had been established by Pope Gregory IX in the first half of the thirteenth century, but it was not until

**LICENCE TO TORTURE in Spain was jointly granted under the auspices of three devout Catholics: Queen Isabella, Gregory IX (centre) and Sixtus IV . . .**

Mansell

Mary Evans

135

Torquemada became involved in it that it really "flourished". Within a few years he had also become the confessor to Ferdinand, and had been appointed the Grand Inquisitor of Spain. It was then that he drew up the 28 main articles of his infamous Code of Terror—itemizing the numerous sins against "Our Lord Jesus Christ", and the punishments they drew.

He stated that, after a warning sermon had been read to the people of a village, town, or city, "the inquisitors shall order to be read and published an admonition with censures against those who are rebellious or who contest the power of the Holy Office". It was desirable to obtain confessions in writing, and he listed the three degrees of suspicion under which someone might fall: the light, the vehement, and the violent.

"Light" offenders could expect such admonitions as fasting, prayers, or pilgrimages. "Vehement" offenders were imprisoned and also made to stand at the door of their principal church bearing candles. "Violent" offenders, providing

they did not recant and so go to prison, were "put to the flame". By burning them in this world, it was reasoned that they would suffer less in the next, and they were told not to "despair".

Some of the articles ranged from the ridiculous—such as No. 27 which stated that anyone who held a "farewell supper" before setting out on a long journey was guilty of heresy—to the malign. Article 9, for example, declared that:

"If any children of heretics . . . should come to seek reconciliation, and to confess the errors they know of themselves, their parents, and any other persons . . . the inquisitors shall receive them kindly, imposing penances lighter than upon others, and shall contrive that these children be tutored in the Faith and the Sacraments of Holy Mother Church."

Article 15 was equally odious. "If the

**SAVAGERY . . . in the name of the Cross! Torquemada's reign of terror marks an all-time low in the checkered history of the Catholic Church's "holy mission".**

said crime of heresy is half-proven, the inquisitors may put the accused to torture, and if under torture he should confess his sin, he must ratify his confession on one of the following three days." Failure to do so allowed the inquisitors to "repeat the torture", and to keep on repeating it until a full and damning confession had been obtained.

Apart from the frequently effective "mental torture", Torquemada sanctioned the use of the rack, the hoist, and the water torture—burning was only used when all else had failed to convert someone to Christ. The racks were of the sort found in most medieval prisons; the hoists were used to raise prisoners to the ceiling and then abruptly drop them so that their arms were almost jerked from their sockets; while the water torture consisted of pouring liquid into a piece of linen attached to the victim's mouth—the weight of the water forced the linen deep into the throat, so that the man endured all the agonies of suffocation without actually dying.

It was the final article, however, which gave Torquemada's men the licence to kill and maim as they chose. "Should any matter arise for which provision has not been made by this code, the inquisitors shall proceed as by law prescribed. It being left to them to dispose as their consciences show them to be best for the service of God and their Highnesses."

Torquemada and his inquisitors— "God-fearing and upright priests, regular or secular, of over 40 years of age"— soon became the most feared and hated men in Spain. For protection, the Grand Inquisitor never ventured abroad without an armed guard of 50 mounted soldiers, and 200 more on foot. All his food and wine was tasted in case it had been poisoned, and the travelling priests were sometimes assassinated—as happened to one in Zaragoza in September 1485, when his killer, Juan Esperandeu, was subsequently hanged, drawn and quartered.

As Torquemada's rule continued—with him building a beautiful monastery for himself, St. Thomas's at Avila, and constructing penitentiaries for the heretics —so the complaints against him grew. Eventually they reached Rome and Pope Alexander VI, who named a number of assistants—granted powers equal to Torquemada's—to "aid" the Grand Inquisitor. The friar objected to this, but failing health restricted him more and more to his monastery.

Crippled with gout, he finally died there in 1498 at the age of 78. For 20 years he had implemented the Latin inscription chiselled on the walls of St. Thomas's— *Pestilence Strike Heretics*—and in doing so had been responsible, to one degree or other, for the deaths of some 2000 "dissenting" people.

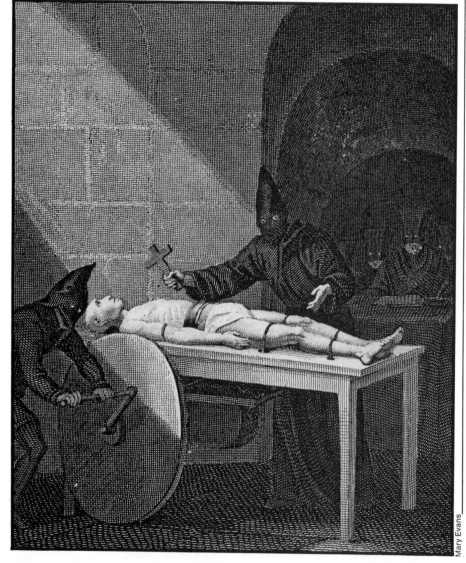

Mary Evans

AS SOON as she learnt that her husband, the Earl of Nithsdale, was to be executed in the Tower of London, his 24-year-old wife, Winifred, decided that he must be saved. Together with her maid, Cecilia Evans, she set out from her home in Dumfries, Scotland, in December 1715. The snow was falling so thickly that the southern-bound stagecoaches had been cancelled, and the two women were forced to journey on horseback. "By the time we reached Stamford, in Lincolnshire," wrote Lady Nithsdale later, "the snow was so deep that our horses were in several places almost buried . . . and we were obliged to continue in the cold that froze our very marrow."

They arrived in London early in January 1716, and were so exhausted from their experience that it was three weeks before they were able to leave their lodgings. Meanwhile they stayed with a "jolly, fat lady—a Mrs. Mills of Drury Lane", and hoped that Lord Nithsdale would be granted a reprieve. Along with five other northern peers, he had been found guilty of treason for his part in the unsuccessful Jacobite uprising of the previous year. The noblemen had attempted to depose the German-born George I from the English throne to make way for James Stuart, the exiled "Old Pretender".

# TOWER OF LONDON

By the middle of February it was clear that Lord Nithsdale would not be spared the executioner's axe. He was due to be beheaded on the 24th of the month, and Lady Nithsdale hurried to St. James's Palace, where she burst into a reception being given by the king. She cornered him in a drawing-room, went down on her knees, grasped his embroidered coat, and wept and pleaded. In his anger, George dragged her halfway across the room before court officials managed to pull her away.

On her return to Drury Lane she realized that it was up to her to "secrete my good lord from his captors". Enlisting the support of Cecilia Evans, Mrs. Mills, and

**THE MOST FORBIDDING of England's prisons, the Tower of London was thought to be impossible to escape from. Lady Nithsdale's initiative proved otherwise.**

a sympathizer named Miss Hilton—"a slender, loyal lady"—she prepared for a visit to the Tower. After warning her husband of her intention, and tactfully bribing his warders, she told Miss Hilton to wear two riding cloaks—one over the other—and Mrs. Mills to wear two dresses.

Only one person at a time was allowed to see Lord Nithsdale in his room in the Lieutenant's House—with its window 60 feet above Water Lane—and the three conspirators went there the evening before the prisoner was to be beheaded. Lady Nithsdale first escorted Miss Hilton into "my poor lord's presence, making sure that she left the chamber a cloak lighter than she entered it". Next it was the turn of Mrs. Mills.

"I went partly downstairs, "Lady Nithsdale recorded, "to meet Mrs. Mills, who held her handkerchief to her face, as was natural for a person going to take a last leave of a friend before his execution; and I desired her to do this that my lord might go out in the same manner. Her eyebrows were inclined to be sandy, and as my lord's were dark and thick, I had prepared some paint to disguise him. I had also got an artificial headdress of the same coloured hair as hers, and rouged his face and cheeks, to conceal his beard.

"All this provision I had before left

in the Tower. The poor guards, who my slight liberality the day before had endeared me to them, let me go out quietly with my company, and were not so strictly on the watch as they usually had been, and the more so as they were persuaded, from what I had told them the day before, that the prisoners [Lords Derwentwater and Kenmure were also due to be executed for their part in the uprising] would obtain their pardon."

With the departure of the two visitors, Lady Nithsdale stayed behind with her husband. It was growing dark by the time she had finished dressing him, and she was frightened that the candlelight might betray them.

So, while the Earl held a handkerchief to his eyes, his wife spoke to him "in the most piteous and afflicted tone, bewailing the negligence of my maid Evans who had ruined me by her delay". On reaching the lower door, she addressed the Earl as "dear Mrs. Betty" and beseeched "her" to quickly go to Drury Lane and bring the maid to the Tower.

Keystone

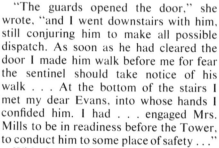

**DISGUISED with the help of his brilliant and courageous wife, Lord Nithsdale evades the watchful gaze of the prison guards. Today the Tower still gives an impression of impregnability (above) which time has not dispelled.**

"The guards opened the door," she wrote, "and I went downstairs with him, still conjuring him to make all possible dispatch. As soon as he had cleared the door I made him walk before me for fear the sentinel should take notice of his walk . . . At the bottom of the stairs I met my dear Evans, into whose hands I confided him. I had . . . engaged Mrs. Mills to be in readiness before the Tower, to conduct him to some place of safety . . ."

With her husband safely out of the Tower, and in a waiting coach, Lady Nithsdale returned to the chamber and proceeded to talk as if her lord was still present. "I spoke to him as it were, and, in my lord's voice as near as I could imitate it, I answered as if he had, and walked up and down as if we were conversing together." She then held the door ajar, bade her husband a solemn and sorrowful good night. As she moved into the passage, and passed the guards, she told them: "I pray you, do not disturb my lord. He is at his prayers."

Within the hour Lady Nithsdale had joined her husband in Drury Lane, where he was hiding in Mrs. Mills' attic. From there he was moved to the house of the Venetian Ambassador—who knew nothing of his presence—and, disguised in the ambassador's livery, he made his way south to Dover. Under the alias of "William Maxwell, a coachman", Lord Nithsdale proceeded to Lille, in France, where he was later reunited with his wife.

His escape from the Tower—which was first built in the eleventh century by William the Conqueror "to protect and control the city"—meant that he and Lady Nithsdale could not return to Britain. They spent 30 happy years living in exile in Rome, and receiving a small pension from the grateful James Stuart. "Had it not been for the cunning and daring of my wife," said the Earl, "I should have ended my life on the executioner's block. I wonder if, in her place. I would have been as courageous?"

Mary Evans

YOUNG Stanley Wilson couldn't, as he said later, "believe his eyes". At a baccarat game at his father's house party—attended by the future King Edward VII of England, the Prince of Wales—one of the players could be seen cheating. Wilson, the son of a north-country ship-owner at whose mansion, Tranby Croft, the guests were gathered, looked again. There was no doubt about it. Each time he thought he was unobserved, Lieutenant-Colonel Sir William Gordon-Cumming—of the Scots Guards—fingered the pile of red £5 counters in front of him, adding to or subtracting from their number.

A white line separated the playing area from the rest of the table, and the object of the game was to be dealt an eight or a nine. As soon as he received such a card, Sir William surreptitiously pushed more of his counters over the line, so increasing his stake. If the dealer didn't "favour" him, then he just as furtively edged his counters back. It was clear that the 42-

# TRANBY CROFT

**ACCUSED OF CHEATING at a house party in the North of England, Sir William Gordon-Cumming (right) was determined to clear his name and took the matter to court—with disastrous results.**

year-old officer must be denounced, but that was not so easily done.

Together with Bertie (as the Prince was popularly known), Sir William had travelled north to attend the 1890 St. Leger horserace, being held at nearby Doncaster in two days' time. They had not previously met their host, although he was well known to their fellow guests, such as the Earl and Countess of Coventry, and General Owen Williams. For a while Stanley Wilson was nonplussed. Then he turned to one of Sir William's subalterns, Berkeley Levett, and whispered: "Keep your eye on Sir William. Dammit, I believe the man is cheating!"

To begin with, Levett dismissed the accusation. Then, to his horror, he saw Sir William hold his clasped hand low over the table and drop two £5 counters onto the cloth. The following night after dinner—and the second night of Bertie's stay—the pattern was repeated. Sir William was no more than a common cheat, and Wilson's brother-in-law, Lycett Green, wrote as much in a note to his hostess, Mrs. Wilson. She knew such "ploys" were practised by the croupiers at Monte Carlo—but she had never known them to be used by a British officer and gentleman.

On the third day, after the party had attended the St. Leger, Mrs. Wilson and Lycett Green called a private meeting with the Prince of Wales. At it Bertie was told about the "low deceit" of his close friend, and in turn he confronted Sir William. "We don't want to be too hard on you," he said. "So do the decent thing and play straight from now on."

Had it been left to Bertie, the affair would have ended there. At the age of 40 he had already been attacked for his loose and frivolous way of life. Baccarat was illegal in the England of 1890, and he did not wish to have yet another scandal associated with his name. However, Lord Coventry and General Williams felt that a friendly warning was not enough. Despite Sir William's anger and protests, they insisted that he signed an undertaking not to play cards—for money or otherwise—again.

"In consideration of the promise, made by the gentlemen whose names are subscribed, to preserve silence with reference to an accusation made regarding my conduct at baccarat on the nights of Monday and Tuesday, September 8 and 9, 1890, at Tranby Croft, I will on my part solemnly undertake never to play cards again as long as I live."

Redfaced with rage and embarrassment, the "blackguard" then packed his bags

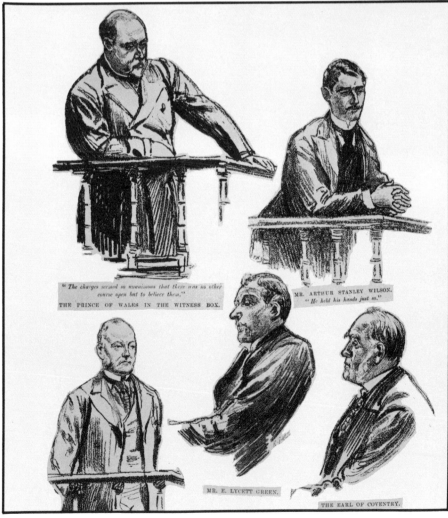

"The charges seemed so unanimous that there was no other course open but to believe them."
THE PRINCE OF WALES IN THE WITNESS BOX.

MR. ARTHUR STANLEY WILSON.
"He held his hands just so."

MR. E. LYCETT GREEN.

THE EARL OF COVENTRY.

**AMONG FELLOW PLAYERS (left) at Tranby Croft was the Prince of Wales. The court case heaped scandal on the Prince as baccarat was illegal at the time . . .**

and left Tranby Croft. The note—which had also been signed by the Prince and nine other guests—was put into the safe-keeping of Bertie's private secretary. The world of fashion and gambling would never have known of the incident had not Sir William—after discussing the whole affair with his Commander-in-Chief, the Duke of Cambridge—decided to "clear his name".

He was prompted to do this by an anonymous letter which he received from Paris early in the following year. It referred to what had taken place at Tranby Croft, and he felt he had no course but to sue his accusers for slander. As a serving officer he was officially unable to bring a civil action. His resignation from the army was blocked, and so he went to the Judge-Advocate General, Sir Redvers Buller, who sanctioned a civil appeal.

"'I hear," said Sir Redvers, "that the Prince is condemning my action . . . in loud and unmeasured terms. I am satisfied that I have fulfilled my duty with

discretion." The action was heard before the Lord Chief Justice, Lord Coleridge, in the first week of June 1891. The Prince of Wales, as a prosecution witness, rarely left the court, and Sir William was defended by the Solicitor-General, Sir Edward Clarke—who was "thoroughly convinced" of his client's innocence.

Claiming that the accused was the victim of a plot to "save the honour" of a Prince who had taken part in an illegal game, Sir Edward told the jury: "There have been plenty of occasions of men willing to sacrifice themselves to support a tottering throne or prop a falling dynasty." The Prince's mother, Queen Victoria, crossly recorded her view that, "It is a fearful humiliation to see the future king of this country dragged through the dirt, just like anyone else, in a court of justice."

**THE BACCARAT CASE . . . Prominent in the courtroom were Mr. Asquith (top left), Lord Edward Somerset (right), Mr. Gill and Mr. Berkeley Levett (left and right).**

The jury, however, did not share her sense of humiliation. On June 9, after an absence of only 15 minutes, they found Sir William Gordon-Cumming guilty of cheating. So Bertie stood morally accused of more than just breaking the law. He had done so with a companion who did not even have what one commentator called "honour among gentlemen thieves". *The Times* thundered that the Prince should also pledge never to play cards again. The Archbishop of Canterbury and the Kaiser joined the attack.

The Kaiser wrote to Queen Victoria protesting that an honorary Colonel in the Prussian Hussars—as Bertie was—should "become embroiled with men young enough to be his children in a gaming squabble". Dismissed from the Army, expelled from his clubs, ostracized by society, Sir William retired to his estate in Scotland—where he died, a forgotten man, in 1930. As for the Prince, he stopped playing baccarat and took up the more socially acceptable game of bridge.

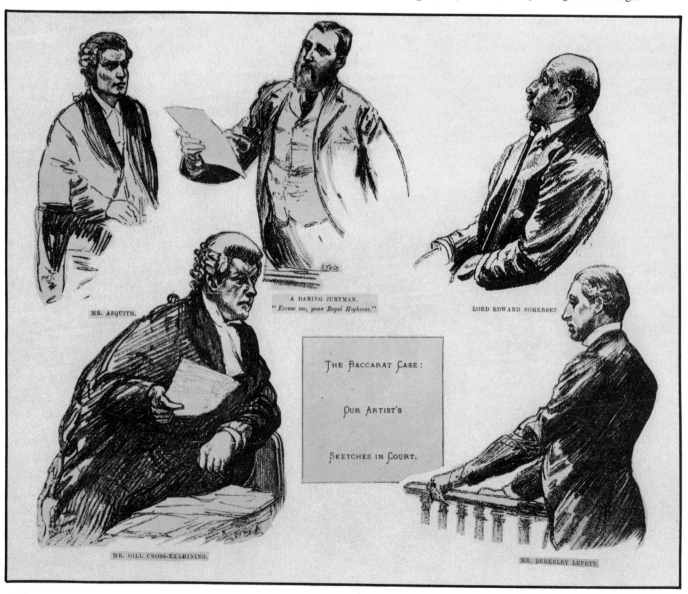

MR. ASQUITH.

A DARING JURYMAN.
"Excuse me, your Royal Highness."

LORD EDWARD SOMERSET.

THE BACCARAT CASE:

OUR ARTIST'S

SKETCHES IN COURT.

MR. GILL CROSS-EXAMINING.

MR. BERKELEY LEVETT.